RAND NATIONAL DEFENSE RESEARCH INSTITUTE

China's Foreign Aid and Government-Sponsored Investment Activities

Scale, Content, Destinations, and Implications

T0302662

Charles Wolf, Jr., Xiao Wang, Eric Warner

The research described in this report was prepared for The Smith Richardson Foundation, The Hoover Institution, and The Bradley Foundation—and by the Director of Net Assessment in the Office of the Secretary of Defense (OSD). The research was conducted within the RAND National Defense Research Institute, a federally funded research and development center sponsored by OSD, the Joint Staff, the Unified Combatant Commands, the Navy, the Marine Corps, the defense agencies, and the defense Intelligence Community.

Library of Congress Control Number: 2013949539

ISBN: 978-0-8330-8128-5

RAND OFFICES

SANTA MONICA, CA • WASHINGTON, DC

PITTSBURGH, PA • NEW ORLEANS, LA • JACKSON, MS • BOSTON, MA

DOHA, QA • CAMBRIDGE, UK • BRUSSELS, BE

www.rand.org

Preface

With the world's second largest economy, China has the capacity to engage in substantial programs of development assistance and government investment in any and all of the emerging market countries. In the first decade of the 21st century, it has expanded and directed this capacity in 93 countries for both the benefit of the recipients and its own interests.

Up until the early 2000s little was known about the extent of China's activities but this has been changing in recent years. Thomas Lum of the Congressional Research Service offered an initial estimate of China's aid and government-sponsored investment activities in Africa, Latin America, and Southeast Asia. This study expands those findings. Using several data sources and aggregation methods, RAND researchers built a database to describe these programs. It assessed the scale, trends, and composition of these programs in six regions: Africa, Latin America, the Middle East, South Asia, Central Asia, and East Asia. Finally, it derived inferences and insights from the analysis that may enhance understanding of these programs and policies pertaining to them.

This research was sponsored by several private institutions—The Smith Richardson Foundation, The Hoover Institution, and The Bradley Foundation—and by the Director of Net Assessment in the Office of the Secretary of Defense. It was conducted within the International Security and Defense Policy Center of the RAND National Security Research Division (NSRD). NSRD conducts research and analysis on defense and national security topics for the U.S. and allied defense, foreign policy, homeland security, and intelligence communities and foundations and other non-governmental organizations that support defense and national security analysis.

For more information on the International Security and Defense Policy Center, see http://www.rand.org/nsrd/ndri/centers/isdp.html or contact the director (contact information is provided on the web page).

Contents

Preface iii
Figures vii
Tables ix
Summary xi
Acknowledgments xvii
Abbreviations xix

CHAPTER ONE
Introduction 1

CHAPTER TWO
Foreign Aid Literature Review 3
Differing Definitions of Aid: OECD and China 3
Academic Literature on Foreign Aid 4
Literature on Chinese Aid: Forms, Scale, and Scope 5
Forms of Chinese FAGIA and Comparison to OECD ODA/ODF 6
Research into the Scale and Scope of Chinese FAGIA 7
Summary 8

CHAPTER THREE
Structure and Management of China's Foreign 'Aid' and Government-Sponsored Investment Activities 11

CHAPTER FOUR
Worldwide Scale, Trends, and Composition of China's FAGIA 17
Pledged and Delivered FAGIA: Scale, Trends, and Assessment 18

CHAPTER FIVE
China's FAGIA in Six Regions and Selected Countries 25
Latin America 25
Pledged and Delivered FAGIA: Scale, Trends, and Assessment 26
Categories and Purposes of FAGIA Projects: Elaboration and Assessment 26
Africa 29
Pledged and Delivered FAGIA: Scale, Trends, and Assessment 29
Categories and Purposes of FAGIA Projects: Elaboration and Assessment 31
Middle East 33
Pledged and Delivered FAGIA: Scale, Trends, and Assessment 33
Categories and Purposes of FAGIA Projects: Elaboration and Assessment 35
South Asia 36
Pledged and Delivered FAGIA: Scale, Trends, and Assessment 36
Categories and Purposes of FAGIA Projects: Elaboration and Assessment 38
Central Asia 39
Pledged and Delivered FAGIA: Scale, Trends, and Assessment 40
Categories and Purposes of FAGIA Projects: Elaboration and Assessment 41
East Asia 43
Pledged and Delivered FAGIA: Scale, Trends, and Assessment 43
Categories and Purposes of FAGIA Projects: Elaboration and Assessment 44

CHAPTER SIX
Inferences, Insights, and Related Issues 47
Future Prospects for China's Foreign FAGIA 51
Some Related Issues: Confucius Institutes and Arms Transfers 53

APPENDIXES
A. Data and Methodology 55
B. International Monetary Fund's International Financial Statistics Data 61

References 67

Figures

S.1. Worldwide Annual and Cumulative Pledged and Delivered FAGIA ... xii
4.1. China's Worldwide FAGIA, Annual and Cumulative Costs, 2001–2011 ... 19
4.2. Worldwide Deliveries as Lagged Function of Pledged Assistance ... 21
4.3. Total FAGIA Shares by Category, Average 2001–2011 ... 22
4.4. Total FAGIA Shares by Category, By Year 2001–2011 ... 23
5.1. Annual and Cumulative Estimates of China's Pledged and Delivered FAGIA to Latin America ... 27
5.2. Annual Pledged Plus Delivered FAGIA Estimates to Latin America by Category, 2001–2011 ... 28
5.3. Annual and Cumulative Estimates of Pledged and Delivered FAGIA to Africa ... 30
5.4. Annual Pledged Plus Delivered FAGIA Estimates to Africa by Category, 2001–2011 ... 31
5.5. Annual and Cumulative Estimates of Pledged and Delivered FAGIA to the Middle East ... 34
5.6. Annual Pledged Plus Delivered FAGIA Estimates to Middle East by Category, 2001–2011 ... 36
5.7. Annual and Cumulative Estimates of Pledged and Delivered FAGIA to South Asia ... 37
5.8. Annual Pledged Plus Delivered FAGIA Estimates to South Asia by Category, 2001–2011 ... 39
5.9. Annual and Cumulative Estimates of Pledged and Delivered FAGIA to Central Asia ... 41
5.10. Annual Pledged Plus Delivered FAGIA Estimates to Central Asia by Category, 2001–2011 ... 42

5.11. Annual and Cumulative Estimates of Pledged and Delivered FAGIA to East Asia.......44
5.12. Annual Pledged Plus Delivered FAGIA Estimates to East Asia by Category, 2001–2011.......46
B.1. Comparison Between RAND's FAGIA Estimates and IMF/World Bank Balance of Payments Data, 2001–2010.......64
B.2. Comparison of the Values of China's Current Account Data and L-N-Delivered Assistance Estimates, 2004–2010.......65
B.3. Comparison of the Trend of China's Current Account Data and L-N-Delivered Assistance Estimates, 2004–2010.......65

Tables

6.1. Largest Recipients of China's Cumulative Pledged FAGIA, 2001–2011 ($ billions) 50
A.1. List of Recipient Countries in the FAGIA Database 59
A.2. Example of Data Entry of China's FAGIA in One Country 60
B.1. Comparison Between RAND FAGIA Estimates and IMF/World Bank Balance of Payments Data, 2001–2010 62

Summary

In the first decade of the 21st century, China greatly expanded the scope of its development-assistance and government investment programs. These programs now support initiatives in more than 90 nations around the world. Yet, until recently, little was known about the size and direction of such programs. Thomas Lum of the Congressional Research Service (CRS) offered an initial estimate of the scope and purpose of China's aid and government-sponsored investment activities in Africa, Latin America, and Southeast Asia.[1] In this report, we expand upon those findings, assessing the scale, trends, and composition of China's foreign aid and government-sponsored investment activities (FAGIA) in Africa, Latin America, the Middle East, South Asia, Central Asia, and East Asia.

We find such programs have burgeoned in recent years, with emphasis on development of increased foreign supplies of energy resources, as well as supplies of ferrous and nonferrous minerals. Loans finance many of these programs and feature substantial subsidization, but are also accompanied by rigorous debt-servicing conditions that distinguish China's foreign aid from the grant financing that characterizes development aid provided by the United States and other nations of the Organization for Economic Co-operation and Development.

[1] Thomas Lum, *China's Assistance and Government-Sponsored Investment Activities in Africa, Latin America, and Southeast Asia*, CRS, 2009.

Defining China's FAGIA, Its Structure, and Its Size

As we consider it, China's FAGIA is broader than development assistance programs conducted by the United States and other nations. Official Chinese sources explicitly distinguish three categories of FAGIA: grants, interest-free loans, and concessional loans. The first two are funded by China's state finances, while the Export-Import Bank of China funds the third. Many of these programs fall below the grant element of at least 25 percent that characterizes foreign aid programs of other nations and also have requirements that goods purchased for them be at least 50 percent of Chinese origin.

Prior to 2000, China's FAGIA was distinctly limited in scale and content, as, indeed, was China's role in the global economy. Since then, several contributors have reshaped the scale, content, and destinations of this aid. As a result of its remarkable and sustained economic growth, China's shares of global trade and global product increased, as did the resources available to expand its FAGIA. Because future growth of the Chinese economy depends on increasing supplies of natural resources, especially energy-related resources, much of China's assistance has sought to help countries developing such resources.

The financial muscle of China's aid is mainly provided by large loans from China's Export-Import Bank, the China Development Bank (CDB), and the China Africa Development Fund (which is within the CDB). Several state-owned enterprises, including China's National Overseas Oil Company, the China National Petroleum Corporation, and the China Petrochemical Company, provide technical and financial support. The FAGIA formal management structure is topped by the Ministry of Commerce, which is responsible to China's State Council, and ultimately to the Standing Committee of the Communist Party's Political Bureau, the pinnacle of decisionmaking power in China. Much remains unknown about this structure, including the precise role of the major state-owned enterprises in the planning, decisionmaking, and operation of China's programs, as well as how independently the CDB operates in providing aid, and what advisory role the Ministry of Defense may have.

To derive an estimate of total FAGIA, we conducted a detailed LexisNexis search of keyword references to China's assistance programs for 2001 to 2011, and also made secondary use of data from CRS and other sources. Altogether, we obtained 1,055 articles for the 93 countries in our study.

Our findings show the scale of these programs is very large—many times larger than the separate grant-aid development assistance programs conducted by the United States, Europe, Japan, and other donor countries (Figure S.1). Newly pledged aid from China was $124.8 billion in 2009, $168.6 billion in 2010, and $189.3 billion in 2011—all far above the $1.7 billion it pledged in 2001. The 2010 and 2011 pledged amounts were equivalent to about 3 percent of China's gross domestic product and were more than twice the size of the officially reported budget of China's Ministry of Defense. This scaling may be misleading because China's FAGIA programs, unlike defense expenditures, are financed by subsidized loans and expected paybacks from them. By way of further comparison, we note that development assistance provided by the U.S. Agency for Development was $8 bil-

Figure S.1
Worldwide Annual and Cumulative Pledged and Delivered FAGIA

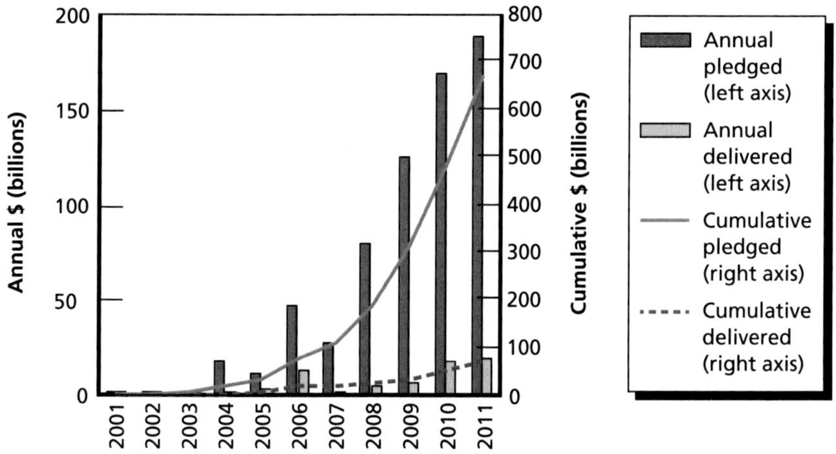

SOURCE: LexisNexis keyword search (See Appendix A).
RAND *RR118-S.1*

lion in 2011 (excluding aid to Iraq and Afghanistan) and that the U.S. Export-Import Bank provided $6.3 billion in worldwide foreign loans in 2011—although, again, we note that China's programs are more broadly defined than most foreign aid programs. Whereas most U.S. foreign aid is provided by grants, China's programs are financed by loans. In consequence, and since we do not know the precise level of subsidization in Chinese official aid and investment, we cannot directly compare Chinese and Western aid figures.

There are two principal explanations for these sharp increases. First, since the 1990s, China has sustained large current account surpluses, between $200 billion and $350 billion annually, increasing its foreign exchange holdings to more than $1.5 trillion, and providing ample financing for expanding both its aid and its foreign investments. Second, China's interest in expanding its foreign sources and supplies of natural resources as a way of sustaining its rapid economic growth has soared.

Actual deliveries of aid lag far behind pledges of assistance; by our estimate, China has delivered only 9.4 percent of the FAGIA it has pledged. This is not surprising: Most of these projects may require five years or more to complete. Indeed, we found that pledges roughly match deliveries made six years later. Furthermore, the annual rate of newly pledged assistance has increased sharply in recent years, increasing the gap (and possible time delay) between aid pledges and deliveries.

FAGIA Purposes

Worldwide, natural-resource development projects were the purpose of 42 percent of pledged FAGIA funds. Infrastructure projects were the purpose of 40 percent, and other projects, including debt forgiveness and humanitarian aid, comprised 18 percent. Infrastructure and natural-resource projects often complement each other; roadway access, for example, may be essential for natural-resource projects. The programs' amounts and purposes also vary by region.

- Latin America received more aid than any other region between 2001 and 2011. Much of this was for a multi-country natural-resource program that included projects in Argentina, Ecuador, Brazil, Chile, and Venezuela. Before 2005, many of the regional programs focused on infrastructure, including power plants, transportation projects, and housing and telecommunications development. China also offered other assistance to two nations in the region that established diplomatic relations with it in the past decade.

- Africa came in second in terms of aid received. Prior to 2004, many of the programs focused on "other" forms, such as debt cancellation and humanitarian aid. But since then, and especially following China-Africa summits in 2003 and 2006, assistance shifted to a mix of natural-resource programs and, especially, infrastructure—including hydropower, road, and railway projects across Africa. As part of China's diplomatic efforts, the programs have also included construction of stadiums and parliamentary buildings. Oil was the purpose of most natural-resource development programs in Africa, but other projects have sought to develop resources of gold, platinum, diamonds, uranium, and aluminum.
- Middle East countries have received aid aimed at financing oil and gas projects, constructing a railway, and debt forgiveness. Most large projects in this region aligned with China's global resource strategy, to search and explore for oil in the Middle East. Most of the "other" forms of assistance have gone to debt forgiveness or cancellation, especially for Iraq.
- FAGIA in South Asia has been unique in focusing on infrastructure and financial aid rather than natural-resource development. There have been two major initiatives: an economic development package signed in 2006 that includes building a seaport, oil refineries, and agricultural advancement; and a $15 billion agreement signed in 2010 for constructing two hydropower projects. Pakistan has received the overwhelming share of assistance in South Asia, to the tune of $89 billion.
- Central Asia received relatively little aid. Most assistance in the region was offered to fund oil, natural gas, and mining projects. In recent years, regional cooperation organizations such as the

Shanghai Cooperation Organisation have played a major role in increasing China's multilateral trade with the region. This has resulted in several major program agreements for regional infrastructure and natural-resource development.

- FAGIA programs in East Asia reflected a more balanced approach than those in other regions (and does not, as we consider it, include in-kind assistance to North Korea). Among North Asian nations, economic development dominated the programs prior to 2006, but infrastructure has since taken over the top spot. Among Southeast Asian nations, infrastructure has accounted for most assistance all along, with the remaining funds focusing on a mix of natural-resource and "other" FAGIA projects. Programs in this region appear to be largely driven by recipient needs, with some exceptions that are complementary with China's interests.

Future Directions

Whether the scale of China's FAGIA will increase, decrease, or remain the same in coming years is unclear. Facing slower economic growth, some policymakers may seek to maintain or even increase the programs as a valuable stimulus for exports. Furthermore, if China's domestic supplies of fossil fuels and key minerals continue to be depleted while industrial demands for them continue to grow, the nation may have incentives to expand its supplies through FAGIA agreements with developing countries and regions. At the same time, competing claimants on domestic, government-financed resources may view reductions of aid as a way to free resources. The People's Liberation Army is one such claimant; others are State Council members concerned with the severe income disparities between the rich, dynamic eastern provinces and the poorer, slower-growing central and western ones. Regardless of future decisions, the pledges China has already made indicate aid deliveries will remain quite large at least for the next several years.

Acknowledgments

The authors express their keen appreciation to Dr. Nicholas Eberstadt from the American Enterprise Institute for discerning, constructive, and helpful comments; to two RAND research librarians, Sachi Yagyu and Anita Szafran, for invaluable assistance in developing and implementing the LexisNexis search methodology we used to build our database; and to two RAND reviewers who provided us with many useful comments and suggestions, but have chosen to remain anonymous. Keith Crane served as another of the internal RAND reviewers. We would also like to express our thanks to Thomas Lum at the Congressional Research Service for his valuable contribution of data to this work; and to the project's informal advisory committee—Professor Harry Rowen, Dr. Greg Treverton, and Dr. Paul Wolfowitz—for their helpful guidance and suggestions. Finally, the authors deeply appreciate the support received from the Smith Richardson Foundation, the Hoover Institution, the Bradley Foundation, and the Office of Net Assessment in the Department of Defense.

All of those named above are absolved of any responsibility for errors of data or mistaken interpretation that may remain in this report.

Abbreviations

AT	arms transfer
CDB	China Development Bank
CNOOC	China's National Overseas Oil Company
CI	Confucius Institutes
CNPC	China National Petroleum Corporation
CRS	Congressional Research Service
FAGIA	foreign aid and government-sponsored investment activities
FDI	foreign direct investment
IIP	International Investment Position
IMF	International Monetary Fund
L-N	LexisNexis
LIBOR	London Interbank Offered Rate
MOFCOM	Ministry of Commerce
NOC	national oil company
ODA	official development assistance
ODF	official development finance

OECD	Organisation for Economic Co-operation and Development
PLA	People's Liberation Army
SCO	Shanghai Cooperation Organisation
SEZ	special economic zones
SINOPEC	China Petrochemical Company
SOE	state-owned enterprise

CHAPTER ONE

Introduction

As China's economy has expanded in recent years, so, too, has its capacity to engage in substantial programs of development assistance. Its foreign aid and government-initiated investment activities have burgeoned in recent years. Yet little has been known about the extent of China's aid activities. Thomas Lum of the Congressional Research Service (CRS) offered an initial estimate of China's aid and government-sponsored investment activities in Africa, Latin America, and Southeast Asia.[1] We seek to build on Lum's work by providing a more complete description of China's foreign aid and government-sponsored investment activities in the first decade of the 21st century, including those in Africa, Latin America, the Middle East, South Asia, Central Asia, and East Asia.

These programs have burgeoned in recent years. They have also emphasized development of increased foreign supplies of energy resources, as well as supplies of ferrous and nonferrous minerals.

It is difficult to make a precise estimate of the cost burden because of several obscurities in the data; e.g., depending on whether the relative prices of natural resource commodities that China receives in repayment of its program loans rise or fall between the time that loan agreements are signed and the time that consigned commodities are delivered to China, the cost burden on China could turn out to be negative (i.e., the value of repayments could exceed the nominal program costs), or it could approach the full value of the original loans; also, depend-

[1] Thomas Lum, *China's Assistance and Government-Sponsored Investment Activities in Africa, Latin America, and Southeast Asia*, CRS, 2009.

ing on the frequency of nonperforming loans or of defaults, the cost burden could amount to the full-dollar costs. In any event, in the short term and the middle term, deliveries made to recipients thereby equivalently reduce the real resources available for meeting other claims for consumption and investment within China.

The loans and loan conditions that provide financing for these programs have had some distinctive characteristics as well. China's loan financing entails substantial subsidization, but is accompanied by rigorous debt-servicing conditions that distinguish China's foreign aid from the grant financing that characterizes development aid provided by the United States and other countries in the Organization for Economic Co-operation and Development (OECD). In particular, China's aid programs, as we consider them, do not conform to OECD and U.S. definitions of what constitutes foreign "aid" in emerging-market countries. These definitions limit use of the term to programs whose grant component is at least 25 percent of "aid."

In assessing China's foreign aid and government-sponsored investment activities (FAGIA), we seek to identify trends over the past decade, to infer priorities among the regions and countries that have received such assistance, and to draw further inferences about its likely future directions and purposes.

To place our discussion in a broader context, in the next chapter we briefly review the literature on foreign aid, covering both OECD and Chinese government agencies, and academic perspectives. In the third chapter, we review the structure and management of China's FAGIA. In the fourth chapter, we present an overview of the worldwide scale, costs, and composition of these programs, using a new data set we constructed for this project and will describe later. (Readers who wish to receive the full data may request it by email to wolf@rand.org, xiaowang@rand.org, or ewarner@rand.org.) In the fifth chapter, we delve deeper into our data to discuss China's programs in the six regions we analyze as well as in some individual countries. We conclude in the sixth chapter with summary insights, inferences we draw from the data, and a review of some directions the Chinese programs may take going forward.

CHAPTER TWO

Foreign Aid Literature Review

The literature on foreign aid is extensive; as a result, any brief review of it will cover only some of the highlights. In this chapter, we focus on concepts and definitions of foreign aid as presented by international organizations and by China, as well as other research on the linkage between foreign aid and economic growth, and previous literature on the scope and scale of China's aid.

Differing Definitions of Aid: OECD and China

The OECD defines two forms of development aid programs:

1. Official development assistance (ODA) consists of technical aid, official grants, or loans promoting economic development and welfare, and having concessional terms, with a grant element of at least 25 percent.[1]
2. Official development finance (ODF) consists of "non-concessional development lending by multilateral financial institutions" and "other official flows for development purposes

[1] The OECD also notes the following exclusions in its aid definition: "Grants, loans and credits for military purposes are excluded. Transfer payments to private individuals (e.g., pensions, reparations or insurance payouts) are in general not counted." See the definition of ODA. OECD, *Development Assistance Committee Glossary of Key Terms and Concepts* web page, undated.

(including refinancing loans) which have too low a grant element to qualify as ODA."

The Information Office's white paper on China's foreign aid lacks a clear definition for comparison with the OECD terminology. It states that its foreign aid represents "mutual help between developing countries, focuses on practical effects, accommodates recipient countries' interests, and strives to promote friendly bilateral relations and mutual benefit through economic and technical cooperation with other developing countries."[2]

Academic Literature on Foreign Aid

Academic literature on foreign aid focuses on a number of areas, including the economic development outcomes of aid in recipient countries and the connections of aid and trade between donor and recipient countries. Empirical studies of the effects of aid on economic development have produced mixed results. Boone found that foreign aid has a positive effect on the size of government, but a negative effect on economic growth and investment.[3] A later empirical study by Burnside and Dollar showed statistically significant effects on economic growth of aid, but only if the recipients had sound trade, fiscal, and monetary policies in place.[4] Using an expanded data set and similar specifications, Easterly, Levine, and Roodman found no evidence that economic development is linked with foreign aid, even in countries with sound economic policies.[5] Later work by Rajan and Subramanian shows that even in varying policy

[2] Information Office of the State Council, "China's Foreign Aid" white paper, Beijing, April 2011.

[3] Peter Boone, "Politics and the Effectiveness of Foreign FAGIA," *European Economic Review*, Vol. 40, No. 2, 1996, pp. 289–329.

[4] Craig Burnside and David Dollar, "Aid, Policies, and Growth," *American Economic Review*, Vol. 90, No. 4, 2000, pp. 847–68; See also William Easterly, Ross Levine, and David Roodman, *New Data, New Doubts: A Comment on Burnside and Dollar's "Aid, Policies, and Growth" (2000)*, National Bureau of Economic Research, 2003.

[5] Easterly, Levine, and Roodman, 2003.

environments and for different types of aid, no combination of the two yielded positive effects upon economic growth.[6] A more recent study by Akramov finds that aid to certain sectors (i.e., agriculture, manufacturing, and mining) and to infrastructure (e.g., transport, communications, and power generation) contribute to economic growth, but aid to "social sectors" (e.g., health and education) do not.[7]

The linkages between trade and aid have also been examined in previous works, with mixed results. Wagner shows that approximately 50 percent of foreign aid in the 1990s was tied with exports.[8] This study also showed that an increase in exports in the amount of 133 percent of total aid is associated with aid disbursements. Research by Lloyd et al. has also shown a linkage between trade and aid, but its direction and magnitude are unknown.[9] Also of note, work by Morrisey and White shows that exports are more beneficial to the recipient countries than tied aid—and under reasonable conditions, are more beneficial than associated finance or low-concessional aid.[10]

Literature on Chinese Aid: Forms, Scale, and Scope

Due to the lack of detailed quantitative data on Chinese FAGIA flows, most prior research on China's programs focused on the forms, impacts,

---

6 G. Raghuram Rajan and Arvind Subramanian, "Aid and Growth: What Does the Cross-Country Evidence Really Show?" NBER Working Paper, No. 11513, Cambridge, Mass.: National Bureau of Economic Research, 2005.

7 Kamiljon T. Akramov, *Foreign Aid Allocation, Governance, and Economic Growth*, International Food Policy Research Institute, 2012.

8 Don Wagner, "Aid and Trade—An Empirical Study," *Journal of the Japanese and International Economies*, Vol. 17, No. 2, 2003, pp. 153–173.

9 Tim Lloyd, Mark McGillivray, Oliver Morrissey, and Robert Osei, "Does Aid Create Trade? An Investigation for European Donors and African Recipients," *European Journal of Development Research*, Vol. 12, No. 1, 2000, pp. 107–123.

10 At the time of this article's publication, associated financing was defined as having a grant element of at least 35 percent; low concessional aid is aid with a grant element of at least 50 percent of the total aid amount. See Oliver Morrisey and Howard White, "Evaluating the Concessionality of Tied Aid," The Manchester School, 1996, pp. 213, 214, 221, 222.

and policies associated with them. It did not examine the scale and scope of Chinese assistance worldwide and among regions.

Forms of Chinese FAGIA and Comparison to OECD ODA/ODF

Both official Chinese sources and previous academic literature examine various forms of Chinese FAGIA. China's programs, as we consider them, have several unique characteristics and are broader than development-assistance programs conducted by the United States, European Union, Japan, and other donor countries.

Official Chinese sources explicitly distinguish three categories of FAGIA: "grants (aid gratis), interest-free loans and concessional loans. The first two come from China's state budgets, while concessional loans are provided by the Export-Import Bank of China as designated by the Chinese government."[11] Grants provided by the Chinese government compare favorably with the OECD definition of ODA. Chinese loan terms are more complicated, however, and require a more detailed comparison.

Several other studies provide explicit descriptions of the types and forms of concessional and interest-free loans that comprise most Chinese programs. The data we collected indicates the average loan extended has been for about $850 million.[12] Previous studies have identified Chinese concessional loan terms, with scheduled drawdowns and repayment over 15 years and an additional five-year grace period.[13] These loan terms clearly reflect subsidization by the lending institu-

[11] Information Office of the State Council, 2011.

[12] Please note that this includes all types of loans included in this study, namely commercial, concessional, and interest-free loans.

[13] Paul Hubbard, *Aiding Transparency: What We Can Learn About China Exim Bank's Concessional Loans,* Center for Global Development, 2007. Hubbard also notes that for 12 loans extended worldwide by the China ExIm Bank, the average interest rate was 2.9 percent. Data collected by Downs for eight loans extended worldwide by the China Development Bank has similar loan terms with interests averaging at 3.3 percent and a ten-year repayment term. This is also consistent with terms as described by Brautigam. See Deborah Brautigam, *The Dragon's Gift: The Real Story of China in Africa*, Oxford, UK: Oxford University Press, 2011; Erica Downs, "Inside China, Inc: China Development Bank's Cross-Border Energy Deals," Brookings Institute, 2011.

tions. Loans for aid purposes may also include collateralization (which may consist of the property and other assets under development) and designation of revenues generated by exports to China of specific commodities, and sometimes they may be tied to procurement of equipment and technical services imported from China. Chinese concessional loans also include a stipulation that at least 50 percent of the loan is tied to the purchase of Chinese goods.[14] These latter requirements permeate Chinese programs, as we discuss further in Chapters Three and Four of this report.

Such conditions attached to China's programs complicate their comparison to "development assistance" as defined by the OECD. As noted above, the OECD definition requires that ODA must have "a grant element of at least 25 percent"[15]—were Chinese FAGIA to fall short of this threshold, the deficient component would register at least as ODF.

Research into the Scale and Scope of Chinese FAGIA

Official Chinese sources provide limited data on levels of Chinese FAGIA.[16] The best examples of prior academic work on China's programs have focused on Africa and include Davies et al. and Brautigam. Both these provide detailed case studies across Africa and annual estimates of Chinese assistance to African nations.[17]

The only work that attempts to estimate regional levels of Chinese assistance as well as relative levels of assistance by type across regions

---

[14] Brautigam, 2011.

[15] Please refer to the previously listed definitions of ODA and ODF.

[16] Examples of such data include the following: "By the end of 2009, China had provided a total of 256.29 billion yuan in aid to foreign countries, including 106.2 billion yuan in grants, 76.54 billion yuan in interest-free loans and 73.55 billion yuan in concessional loans." (Note that there is no start date for these statistics, nor an indication if these are current-year or deflated figures.) Information Office of the State Council, 2011.

[17] Martyn Davies, Hannah Edinger, Nastasya Tay, and Sanusha Naidu, "How China Delivers Development Assistance to Africa," Centre for Chinese Studies, University of Stellenbosch, 2008; Brautigam, 2011.

has been done by CRS.[18] Their reports use data developed through searches of media sources describing Chinese programs, as no official database exists. Additionally, these reports only consider China's programs from 2000 to 2007 in three regions. Our report draws heavily upon the initial data collection efforts by CRS, while expanding data on China's programs to include data from 2001 to 2011 over a larger set of recipient countries in six regions.

Summary

In this brief literature review, we have sought to cover several broad issues, including formal definitions of aid and comparisons to Chinese forms of aid; prior academic literature on foreign aid; and previous measurement of the scale and scope of Chinese FAGIA.

The OECD definition indicates that, to qualify as ODA, aid funding must have "a grant element of at least 25 percent." The loans and other investments that comprise most of China's programs have lower grant elements than this percentage, and hence would more appropriately be considered ODF.

The prior literature on foreign aid covers the relationship between foreign aid and economic development, including the linkage between aid and trade, as well as previous research on Chinese foreign aid. Earlier literature on the economic development effects of aid in recipient countries yielded mixed and inconclusive results, while more recent papers have shown no statistically significant linkage between these two variables. Research on the connection between aid and trade has also been mixed, with some prior research showing a significant boost to trade from aid, while other papers have not been able to determine the direction or magnitude of effects. This research has shown that Chinese assistance follows international norms of limiting (i.e., tying) aid to exports from donor countries to recipient countries.

---

[18] This work includes Lum, 2009; and Thomas Lum, Hannah Fischer, Julissa Gomez-Granger, and Anne Leland, *China's Foreign Aid Activities in Africa, Latin America, and Southeast Asia*, Congressional Research Service, 2009.

Data on relevant foreign transactions from official Chinese sources are lacking. Such official publications provide only broad accounts of the programs without quantitative details. Moreover, the information that is provided does not include any detailed breakdown by the type and purposes of financing by country or over time.

Prior efforts to measure relevant foreign flows for China were hampered by availability of data. The CRS's efforts to estimate Chinese FAGIA to the developing world were among the first such attempts, and that work included data from 2002 to 2007 for three regions: Africa, Southeast Asia, and Latin America. The CRS estimate of total Chinese aid to these three regions over this time period was $74.7 billion. Africa accounted for 44 percent of this total, Latin America for 36 percent, and Southeast Asia for the remaining 20 percent.

We extend the CRS findings to include new regions—the Middle East, South Asia, and Central Asia—and to evaluate China's FAGIA through 2011. Our primary contribution is in expanding this previous study to provide better understanding of the scale and scope of Chinese aid to the developing world. We discuss the evident Chinese objective of obtaining increased supplies of natural resources (especially energy-related resources, but also those relating to ferrous and nonferrous metals), but we do not address other plausible or potential objectives that may motivate China's FAGIA. Such additional motivations may include enhancing China's influence abroad, increasing its access to foreign markets and ports of call. These and other issues remain to be addressed by future research.

CHAPTER THREE

Structure and Management of China's Foreign 'Aid' and Government-Sponsored Investment Activities

Prior to 2000, China's FAGIA was distinctly limited in scale and content, as indeed was China's role in the global economy. Thereafter, several factors contributed to the major changes that ensued in the scale, content, and destinations of China's programs. As a result of its remarkably high and sustained rate of GDP growth (9–10 percent annual real rate of growth in the two preceding decades), China's shares of global trade and of global product waxed, as did its available financial resources for aid expansion. China's policymakers, and the successive leadership of Jiang Zemin and Zhu Rongji, and of Hu Jintao and Wen Jiaobao from the late 1990s through 2012, viewed the economy's sustained high growth as dependent on increasing supplies of natural resources, especially energy-related resources, but also ferrous metals, copper, tin, aluminum, and other metals. The expanded scale and much of the content of China's recent aid programs have resulted from these considerations.

The financial muscle of China's assistance is mainly provided by large loans from China's Export-Import Bank, the China Development Bank (CDB), and the China African Development Fund (within the CDB). This financing both provides and is supplemented by technical and financial support from major state-owned enterprises (SOEs)—such as China's National Overseas Oil Company (CNOOC), the China National Petroleum Corporation (CNPC), and the China Petrochemical Company (SINOPEC)—where the development of natural resources is involved.

At the top of the FAGIA formal management structure is the Ministry of Commerce (MOFCOM), which is responsible to China's State Council and, ultimately, to the Standing Committee of the Communist Party's Political Bureau, the pinnacle of decisionmaking power in China.

The current Minister of Commerce, Gao Hucheng, is an experienced member of the State Council, having previously served as a senior official in the Ministry of Commerce. China's Ministry of Foreign Affairs and its Ministry of Finance are also involved in this chain of command, reflecting the expanded global reach of aid programs since the start of the 21st century.

This description of the management structure omits as much as it includes. For example, the role of the major SOEs in the planning, decisionmaking, and operation of China's programs is unclear, but it probably varies from minimal to decisive in particular projects and countries. Furthermore, the CDB itself is virtually an independent fiefdom reporting directly to the State Council and to the Politburo's Standing Committee, apart from MOFCOM's formal oversight role. It is also unclear whether or how China's Ministry of Defense and the armed forces (People's Liberation Army, or PLA) may play an advisory role or may influence decisionmaking concerning the types of aid that are chosen and the countries where they are located.

This account of the management structure is based on the limited evidence provided by Chinese government and nongovernment sources.[1] In contrast to the abundant information about U.S. foreign assistance programs, past and present, the Chinese government does not publish any comparable documentation pertaining to its programs. It is neither surprising nor unprecedented that the organization and management of these programs are less transparent than comparable programs conducted by other countries.

Granting these limitations, some information is available about the loan financing that undergirds these programs. According to our data and prior studies, the average loan extended by the lending insti-

---

[1] Information Office of the State Council, 2011; interviews with Chinese scholars, officials and others, China and Santa Monica, Calif., December 2011.

tutions mentioned above has been $850 million, with scheduled drawdowns and repayment over 15 years, plus an additional grace period of five years.[2] In many instances, individual countries receive several such loans to support separate projects.

These loan terms clearly reflect subsidization by the lending institutions, reminiscent of what were termed "policy loans" extended by China's state banks to special economic zones (SEZs) in the 1980s and 1990s to spur China's domestic economic growth. Estimating the precise amount of subsidization in China's programs is difficult.[3] Most of the 93 recipients of China's assistance loans would be unable to qualify for long-term loans on the international capital market, regardless of interest rates.[4] On the other hand, several of the principal country recipients with relatively favorable credit ratings would probably be able to borrow at rates perhaps 2–3 percent above the London Interbank Offered Rate (LIBOR),[5] while others would have to pay 4–5 percent above that benchmark, and still others would fail to qualify at any rate.[6] Aggregating over the entire set of recipients, we judge that a con-

---

2 Brautigam, 2011.

3 Regarding costs of the concessional loans: "At present, the annual interest rate of China's concessional loans is between 2% and 3%, and the period of repayment is usually 15 to 20 years (including five to seven years of grace)." Information Office of the State Council, 2011.

4 See Appendix Table A.1 for the list of recipient countries, most of which would be unlikely to qualify.

5 Such recipients include Brazil, Indonesia, and Thailand; see Table 6.1 for a list of the largest individual country recipients.

6 In support of this rough estimate, it is worth noting that the International Monetary Fund (IMF) charged its members—including many of the Fund's member countries, such as recipients of Chinese FAGIA—interest rates between 4.7 percent and 8 percent during the 2007–2011 period for short-term "adjustment" loans, along with unspecified "reduced rates under (its) poverty reduction programs." IMF, *SDR Interest Rate Calculation* web page, undated. The SDR rate includes allowance for exchange rate risk, as well as payback, because of the basket of currencies in the SDR unit. For reference purposes, it is also worth mentioning that Spain's sovereign debt carried interest rates 3–4 percent above LIBOR. We deliberately ignore the investigation by the SEC and other regulatory bodies of possible collusive fraud by key London-based banks to peg LIBOR below a truly market-based estimate of the opportunity cost of capital. See "Timeline: Libor-Fixing Scandal," *BBC*, February 6, 2013.

servative (i.e., "low") estimate of subsidization would perhaps be 3 percent—about equal to the nominal rate of FAGIA loans.[7]

Some of these loans may also include collateralization (consisting of the property and other assets under development) along with designation of revenues generated by exports to China of specific commodities produced by the corresponding assistance projects. The loan agreements typically establish escrow accounts held by the lending institutions, into which export revenues resulting from the assistance projects are deposited and from which the lending institutions withdraw interest and principal for debt servicing, fees, and other payments due to contractors.

In sum, the management of China's FAGIA features commitments made by China and obligations accepted by recipients, costs incurred by China and assets acquired by recipient countries, and concrete benefits expected from the programs by China and other benefits expected by recipients.[8] There is thus a distinctive *quid pro quo* characteristic attached to China's programs. Utilization of FAGIA loans is tied to procurement of equipment and technical services imported from China, and expanded commodity production generated by the assistance projects is explicitly designated for export to China. Much foreign aid from other countries is also tied to procurement; hence, China's practice here is not markedly different. Nevertheless, assuming that, in the absence of tied aid, equivalent procurement could be obtained at lower prices on the open market, it follows that the market-based valuation of tied aid would be somewhat lower than its nominal value.

Although the conditions attached to the programs impose obligations on recipients, these conditions entail risks for the Chinese lenders as well: For example, drawings on the loans may proceed more rapidly

---

7 Another source of uncertainty is attached to this estimate. As noted in the text above, service of the loans is largely accomplished by the revenues from exports generated by the FAGIA projects and consigned to China. It is not entirely clear from the loan agreements whether these revenues are to be calculated at the commodity prices prevailing at the time of the exports, or at the time when the agreements were signed.

8 See, for example, Information Office of the State Council, 2011, pp. 2–3. It repeatedly refers to "mutual benefits" realized by both China and recipients.

than progress on the projects for which the loans were made; or progress on the projects may proceed at a moderate pace, but production of the project's intended commodity exports to China may lag. As commodity production rises, there may also be "leakages" of exports to countries other than China and unintended by China. And, of course, the quantities and value of output from the aid projects may be insufficient to service the loan drawings. A related risk is the possible difference between commodity prices prevailing at the time when a recipient country produces its compensatory exports to China, and the prices at which the original loan terms were negotiated.

CHAPTER FOUR

Worldwide Scale, Trends, and Composition of China's FAGIA

Although MOFCOM publishes considerable information about some of the operational details of individual assistance projects, none of this information covers their costs. Published information describes micro-details about projects relating, for example, to numbers of earth-moving equipment, forklifts, electric generators, computers, technicians, and other project personnel. But this information does not provide the market value of these project inputs—whether expressed in renminbi, dollars, or in the recipients' own currencies.

Part of the explanation for these anomalies may lie in an historical legacy. China's earliest ventures in foreign development assistance occurred in the 1970s and 1980s when these programs were used to counter and to outbid Taiwan's efforts to obtain diplomatic recognition from several smaller nations around the world. Under these circumstances, Beijing was anxious to conceal the amounts of its offers of assistance in order to avoid inflating the ongoing bidding competition with Taiwan. Another part of the explanation may simply be the marked tendency of the Chinese government to limit information that is publicly available on many government activities by over-classifying it—behavior that is characteristic of other governments as well.

The estimates of program costs presented in this report rely principally on a detailed LexisNexis (L-N) search of keyword references to China's assistance programs in 93 countries, and approximately 5,900 media sources around the world, covering the period from 2001 to 2011,[1] and also make secondary use of data from CRS and other sources.[2]

Pledged and Delivered FAGIA: Scale, Trends, and Assessment

The *scale* of China's FAGIA is very large—many times larger than the separate, grant-aid development assistance programs conducted by the United States, Europe, Japan, and other donor countries. China's FAGIA falls within the bounds of its total foreign transfers.[3]

As shown in Figure 4.1, newly *pledged* Chinese aid for the six regions and 93 recipient countries amounted to $124.8 billion in 2009, $168.6 billion in 2010, and $189.3 billion in 2011. In 2010 and 2011, these amounts were equivalent to about 3 percent of China's GDP, and were more than twice as large as the officially reported budget of China's Ministry of Defense.[4] By way of further comparison, we note that development assistance provided by the U.S. Agency for International Development was $8 billion in 2011 (excluding aid to Iraq and Afghanistan) and that the U.S. Export-Import Bank provided $6.3 billion in worldwide foreign loans in 2011.[5] Since we do not know the

---

[1] Appendix A summarizes the sources and methodology used in our estimates. Although the database built for this study is invaluable, it is not without shortcomings. For example, some reported FAGIA pledges might have lapsed, while other pledges may have been missed by the L-N sources. Some delivered assistance may occasionally include double-counting. Still other reported assistance (whether pledged or delivered) may have misstated the actual amounts.

[2] Preexisting data were drawn primarily from those assembled by Thomas Lum at CRS. Lum, 2009.

[3] Appendix B systematically compares our data on deliveries and pledges of Chinese FAGIA with IMF and World Bank time series data on transfers, foreign direct investment (FDI), and loans (omitting from the latter "exceptional financing").

[4] China's officially reported defense budgets in 2010 and 2011 were $76 billion and $90 billion, respectively. International Institute for Strategic Studies, *The Military Balance*, 2012.

[5] See U.S. Export-Import Bank, *Annual Report*, 2011.

Figure 4.1
China's Worldwide FAGIA, Annual and Cumulative Costs, 2001–2011

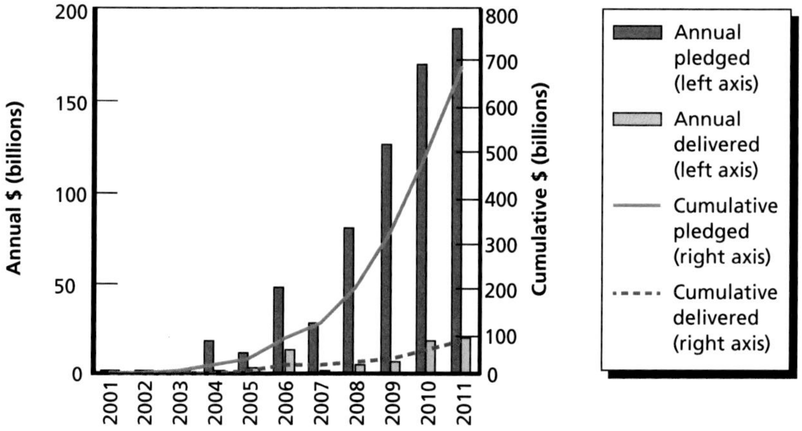

SOURCE: L-N keyword search (See Appendix A).
RAND *RR118-4.1*

precise level of subsidization in Chinese official aid and investment, however, we cannot directly compare Chinese and Western aid figures.

Between 2001 and 2011, China's worldwide pledged aid increased from $1.7 billion to $189 billion annually. The average annual pledged amount during the period was $61 billion, and the average increase was $19 billion annually (albeit with some volatile changes from year to year).[6] Cumulative aid pledged worldwide by China in the 2001–2011 period was $671.1 billion (see Figure 4.1).

There are two principal explanations for these sharp increases. First, China has sustained large current account surpluses since the 1990s, between $200 billion and $350 billion annually, increasing its foreign exchange holdings to more than $1.5 trillion and providing ample financing for expanding both its aid and its foreign investments.[7] Second, China's interest in expanding its foreign sources and

---

6 The annual changes of the 11-year estimates vary from –59 percent to tenfold increases.

7 See Charles Wolf, Jr., Brian G. Chow, Gregory S. Jones, and Scott Harold, *China's Expanding Role in Global Merger and Acquisitions Markets*, Santa Monica, Calif.: RAND Corporation, MG-1162-CAPP, 2011, pp. 2–3.

supplies of natural resources as a way of sustaining its rapid economic growth has soared. Notwithstanding a recent slowing of this growth, the means and the ends of China's FAGIA loans continue to be strong.

To estimate *delivered* aid, as distinct from pledges, we rely on the L-N sources previously mentioned.[8] Figure 4.1 also summarizes our estimates of China's delivered assistance. From 2001 to 2011, our L-N sources indicate average annual worldwide deliveries for FAGIA were $6.3 billion. Cumulative worldwide deliveries through 2010 were $50 billion. Estimated deliveries using the L-N method comprised 9.4 percent of China's total pledged assistance during the decade.

That deliveries amounted to these modest percentages of total pledged assistance isn't surprising; most aid projects require five years or more to complete. Furthermore, the annual rate of newly pledged assistance has risen sharply in recent years; China's pledged assistance between 2009 and 2011 comprised 71 percent of all assistance pledged since 2001, and most of this recent increase would be expected to generate deliveries in later years.

It's also worth noting that the assistance programs don't impose a burden on China's economy until the credit lines are drawn down to pay for the recipients' imports from China that are required for specific development projects. Figure 4.1 also shows the rate at which deliveries have been running in comparison to pledged assistance.

It is to be expected that deliveries will lag behind pledged aid because of technical and logistical considerations relating to the design and implementation of the projects, quite apart from any other causes of the gap between pledges and deliveries. Figure 4.2 illustrates this point by showing the trajectory of deliveries between 2007 and 2011 as a six-year lagged-function of aid pledged between 2001 and 2005, with near convergence reached between pledges made during 2001–2004 and deliveries accomplished by 2010.

Assessing the impact of aid deliveries and pledges on China's economy involves a complex mixture of benefits and opportunities on the one hand, and costs and risks on the other. The positive side of the ledger for China includes several benefits: a welcome stimulus pro-

---

[8] See Appendix A.

Figure 4.2
Worldwide Deliveries as Lagged Function of Pledged Assistance

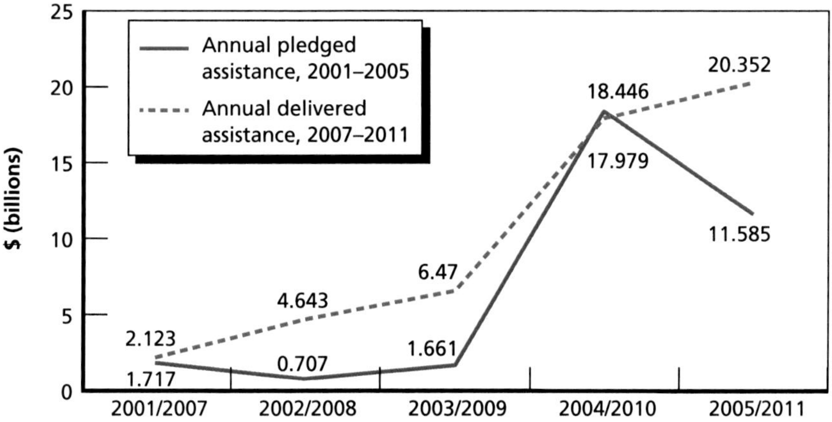

SOURCE: L-N keyword search (See Appendix A).
RAND *RR118-4.2*

vided by FAGIA for China's exports as the economy's remarkable prior growth faces an evident recent slowdown; the prospective increased supplies of key materials and resources to meet the future demands of China's industries; and the hedge that these consigned aid supplies provide in the event of tighter availabilities and higher prices from other sources.

The negative side of the ledger includes possibly added inflationary pressures on top of the 2–3 percent recent annual inflation rate; risks attendant to possible insufficiency of additional exports from aid recipients to service their debts to China; and a possible decline in the relative prices of these commodities in global markets. Our assessment doesn't yield a clear and simple bottom-line for the balance between these pluses and minuses.

We turn next to the *composition* of FAGIA, construed in terms of the categories and purposes identified with the component projects. As shown in Figures 4.3 and 4.4, the predominant projects are divided among: (a) natural resources, consisting principally of energy-related projects (e.g., oil, gas, and coal), and mining of minerals and metals (e.g., copper, ferrous and nonferrous metals); (b) infrastructure (includ-

Figure 4.3
Total FAGIA Shares by Category, Average 2001–2011

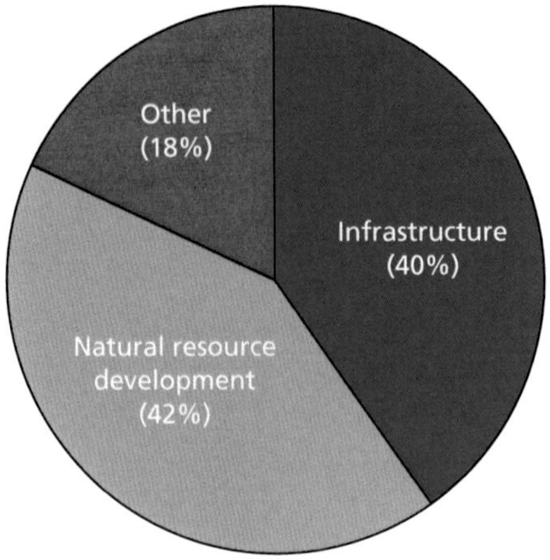

RAND *RR118-4.3*

ing roads, ports, electric power, and schools); and (c) "all other" (consisting *inter alia* of recipients' sovereign debt acquired or forgiven by China, technical assistance, humanitarian assistance, "in-kind" aid, educational and "cultural" assistance).

The precise meanings of, and relationships among, the categories are not reflected in Figures 4.3 and 4.4, and are not entirely clear in the sources on which the figures are based. In theory, "infrastructure" consists principally of public goods possessing the essential characteristics that define their "publicness," and that distinguish them from private goods: Specifically, public goods are *non-rivalrous*, *non-excludable*, and *non-appropriable*.[9] Consequently, pure public goods, such as national security or clean air, are ones to which property rights cannot be

---

[9] See, among others, Gregory Mankiw, *Macroeconomics*, Worth Publishers, 2012; and Charles Wolf, Jr., *Markets or Governments: Choosing Between Imperfect Alternatives*, MIT Press, 1993. "Non-rivalrous" refers to those goods whose benefits are realized collectively by the public at large (e.g., clean air, national security), rather than by individually competing buyers (e.g., cars or books). "Non-excludable" means that producers cannot exclude additional beneficiaries from receiving the benefits, whereas the purchase by a consumer of a private good excludes another consumer from that particular product. "Non-appropriable"

Figure 4.4
Total FAGIA Shares by Category, By Year 2001–2011

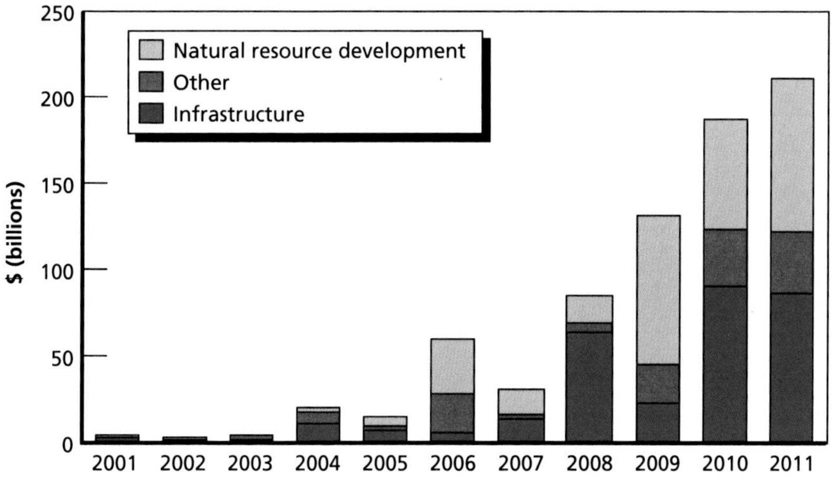

RAND *RR118-4.4*

attached, nor can market-based prices be estimated. It is also true that many projects that fall within the infrastructure category do not meet these criteria. Some infrastructure projects are closely complementary to natural-resource projects, for example—roadway access is essential for many resource projects to proceed, and port development is necessary for assembling, warehousing, and exporting natural-resource commodities (which are inherently private, rather than public, goods). This complementarity is suggested by evidence that infrastructure projects predominated in the first half of the 2001–2011 period (see Figure 4.4), thereby paving the way for subsequent projects to focus on natural-resource development, which predominated in the second half of the period.

Another aspect of the relationship between infrastructure and resource development reflects the negotiatory or bargaining interactions between China and the dozens of aid recipients. Some part of what is

means that, as a consequence of non-excludability, producers can't levy fees on the beneficiaries of public goods.

included as infrastructure (e.g., schools, housing, urban development, stadiums) probably reflects the priorities of aid recipients rather than those of the Chinese donor, while the natural-resource developments are probably more direct reflections of the Chinese developer's priorities. Benefits and obligations associated with the programs accrue to both sides of the transactions.

Finally, in assessing the project categories comprising FAGIA, we should recall the earlier reference to the differing risks they entail for the Chinese donor. For example, where major infrastructure costs are associated with resource development, it is likely that loan drawdowns will be much larger and much earlier than compensatory exports to China of the energy resources or mineral resources produced by the corresponding projects. As between infrastructure and resource projects, it is also likely that importing countries other than China—and unintended and undesired by China (perhaps including the United States)—are more likely to benefit from the resource projects than from the infrastructure projects.

Considering the project composition of the programs in each country and region, it is reasonable to expect a net positive balance between benefits and costs both for China and for its aid recipients. The size of the two-sided balance is likely to vary over time, and also to vary in the assessments made by the respective parties. We do not attempt to assess these two-sided balances in this study.

CHAPTER FIVE

China's FAGIA in Six Regions and Selected Countries

Indicative of the differing purposes and priorities that underlie China's FAGIA programs is their respective size and project composition in six regions and the countries within them. In this chapter, we disaggregate the worldwide data among six regions: Latin America, Africa, Middle East, South Asia, Central Asia, and East Asia. For each region, we first assess the scale and trends of pledged and delivered assistance, then discuss the categories and purposes of China's programs.

Latin America

The 14 countries in Latin America received the largest amount of aid of any region covered in this study. Latin America also received the largest share of natural-resource projects among all regions between 2001 and 2011. Most assistance to Latin America was delivered between 2009 and 2011 in a major global push by China for natural-resource projects. Unlike its engagement in other regions, China does not have the multilateral frameworks of organizations such as the Shanghai Cooperation Organization in Asia and the China-Africa Summit in Africa to facilitate its relationships within Latin America. Chinese engagement there is concentrated on four resource-rich countries: Venezuela, Brazil, Argentina, and Ecuador.

Pledged and Delivered FAGIA: Scale, Trends, and Assessment

Pledged FAGIA

Ninety-five percent of China's aid to Latin America between 2001 and 2011 was pledged after 2008 (the red bars in Figure 5.1); it increased 80-fold in 2009. It increased again in 2010, to approximately $80 billion. This increase was driven by a multicountry natural-resource investment program that included projects in Argentina, Ecuador, Brazil, Chile, and Venezuela.

Delivered FAGIA

Trends in delivered aid approximately follow those of pledged trends. Between 2001 and 2004, Latin America did not receive any delivered aid. The first aid deliveries to the region occurred in 2005, with peaks of $11 billion in 2006 and of $6.6 billion in 2010.

Assessment

As in other regions, most Latin American assistance was in the form of pledged funds. This reflects the growth of natural-resource projects in Latin America between 2006 and 2011. These projects were funded by long-term investments from Chinese mineral companies and loans. Major investors include China's three national oil companies (NOCs): SINOPEC, CNOOC, and CNPC. Loans were primarily provided by China's two policy banks: the CDB and the Export-Import Bank. These loans were for oil: Funds from the CDB were used to finance infrastructure projects throughout Venezuela and would be repaid with future oil deliveries.[1]

Categories and Purposes of FAGIA Projects: Elaboration and Assessment

Natural-resource development dominated Chinese engagement and programs with Latin America between 2001 and 2011. Altogether, Latin America received 44 percent of Chinese assistance for natural-resource development. The mix of assistance (both pledged and delivered) for Latin America has changed greatly over time (Figure 5.2). Prior

---

[1] Simon Hall and Xu Wan, "CNPC, SINOPEC, CNOOC Sign Venezuela O&G Deals," *Dow Jones Newswires*, December 3, 2010.

Figure 5.1
Annual and Cumulative Estimates of China's Pledged and Delivered FAGIA to Latin America

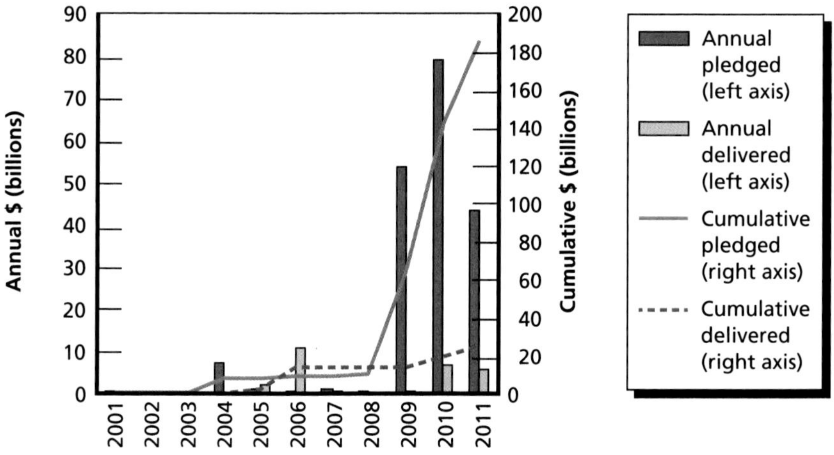

RAND *RR118-5.1*

to 2005, most aid was focused on infrastructure. Since then, natural-resource development projects have dominated Chinese engagement with the region.

While natural-resource projects focused primarily on the development of oil resources, other opportunities also received attention. For example, $3.2 billion went for pledged copper investments in Chile and Ecuador and $4.2 billion for pledged iron-ore investments in Chile, Brazil, and Argentina.

Pledged and delivered infrastructure assistance was distributed across a variety of projects. Approximately one-third of the total number of infrastructure projects (amounting to $5.7 billion) provided traditional, hydro-, and thermal power plants to several Latin American nations. The remaining projects focused on transportation and included railways, transportation hubs, and housing and telecommunications development. As we will note when describing FAGIA in Africa, these programs seemed to reflect infrastructure needs of the recipient country rather than pipelines or railways to bring natural-resource supplies to market.

Figure 5.2
Annual Pledged Plus Delivered FAGIA Estimates to Latin America by Category, 2001–2011

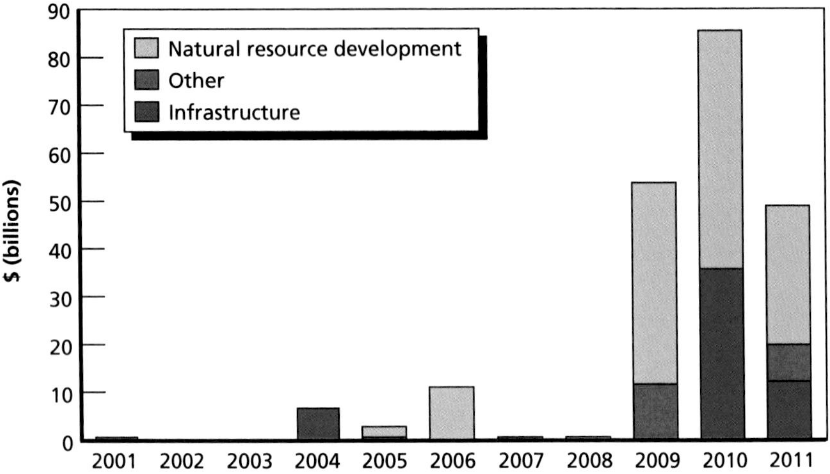

RAND *RR118-5.2*

FAGIA projects in Latin America that were outside the fields of resources and infrastructure development—that is, the "other" category of projects—included trade development, humanitarian assistance, and technical assistance. Of particular note was assistance to Dominica in 2005 and Costa Rica in 2007, closely following each country's diplomatic recognition of the People's Republic of China and severing of ties with Taiwan.[2] Dominica was pledged $122 million in 2005 and Costa Rica $380 million in 2007, the only assistance either country was pledged between 2001 and 2011.

Assessment

Interactions between these programs can be appropriately characterized as mutually beneficial. Examples include a $12 billion agreement between the CDB and Venezuela and a $10 billion loan from the CDB

[2] "China Establishes Diplomatic Relations with the Commonwealth of Dominica," Ministry of Foreign Affairs of the People's Republic of China, March 30, 2004; "China, Costa Rica Set Up Diplomatic Ties," *China Daily*, June 26, 2007.

to the Brazilian NOC Petrobras to be used for further exploration.[3] Other, more unconventional examples were Chinese loans to the Brazilian mining firm Vale to fund construction of ships intended for transporting iron ore to China.

Africa

Between 2001 and 2011, 49 countries in Africa received approximately $175 billion dollars in pledged assistance, making it the second largest regional recipient of aid behind Latin America with $186 billion.

Overall Chinese interaction with Africa during this time reflected both political and economic interests displayed in triennial China-Africa summits. Chinese engagement throughout the region grew steadily, peaked in 2008, and declined between 2009 and 2011. Infrastructure and natural-resource development programs were the two largest categories of aid in Africa. Among African nations, Nigeria received the largest amount of aid during this period.

Pledged and Delivered FAGIA: Scale, Trends, and Assessment

Pledged FAGIA

Overall pledged assistance to Africa changed dramatically between 2001 and 2011 (the red bars in Figure 5.3). Cumulative pledged assistance increased rapidly, from $22 million in 2001 to $175 billion in 2011. Pledged assistance increased on average by approximately $18 billion per year, with large variation among years. There were particularly large increases in 2007 and 2008, after which pledged assistance declined from 2009 to 2011.

Delivered FAGIA

Cumulative delivered aid increased from $52 million in 2001 to $18.4 billion in 2011, an annual average increase of approximately $1.84 billion. Annual growth rates of delivered aid fluctuated during this period, with large increases in 2003, 2006, 2008, and 2010. Two of

[3] "CDB, SINOPEC and Petrobras Sign $10 Billion Loan-for-Oil Contract," *Global Times*, May 26, 2010.

Figure 5.3
Annual and Cumulative Estimates of Pledged and Delivered FAGIA to Africa

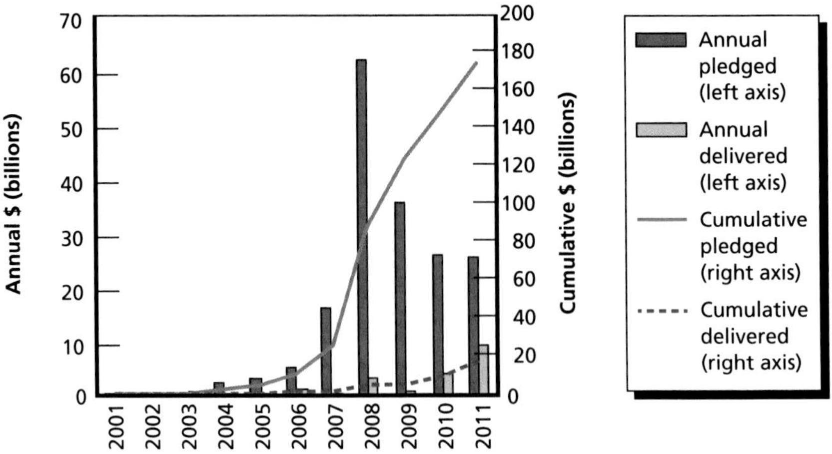

RAND *RR118-5.3*

these large increases occurred in the same year as the triennial China-Africa summits.

Assessment

As in other regions, most FAGIA funding consigned to Africa between 2001 and 2011 was pledged, rather than delivered. Nevertheless, there were two notable points about the rates of delivered funds. First, Africa had the third highest cumulative delivered rate of the regions surveyed, following Central Asia and Latin America. Second, initial assistance to Africa consisted primarily of delivered aid. Prior to 2004, annual delivered assistance averaged 75 percent of total aid. Approximately 97 percent of these delivered funds were applied to debt cancellation projects in African countries. In 2004 there was an increase in pledged aid, primarily due to the shift from other forms of assistance to loan-financed infrastructure and natural-resource development projects, associated with longer lead times between pledges and deliveries. These loans were likely a consequence of the 2003 and 2006 China-Africa summits.

Categories and Purposes of FAGIA Projects: Elaboration and Assessment

Chinese engagement with Africa has undergone major shifts (see Figure 5.4). From 2001 to 2003, pledged and delivered assistance to Africa focused on "other" forms, such as debt cancellation and humanitarian aid. Following China-Africa summits in 2003 and 2006, aid shifted to a mix of natural-resource programs and, especially, infrastructure.

Infrastructure projects were a focus for programs both to Africa and worldwide from 2001 to 2011. From 2005 to 2009, pledged and delivered infrastructure disbursements to Africa accounted for almost 80 percent of worldwide FAGIA infrastructure projects. Of particular note were infrastructure-development programs in Africa in 2008, which accounted for nearly 90 percent of China's worldwide infrastructure disbursements that year. Infrastructure projects varied across countries in the region, depending largely upon the development priorities of the recipient country. Infrastructure projects included 17 dam and hydropower, 19 road, and 17 railway projects throughout Africa.

Figure 5.4
Annual Pledged Plus Delivered FAGIA Estimates to Africa by Category, 2001–2011

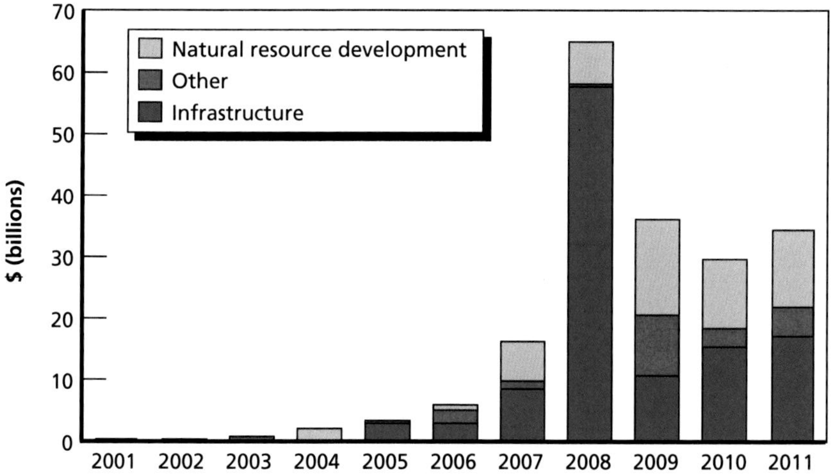

RAND *RR118-5.4*

Other infrastructure projects included four hospitals and three schools. As part of China's diplomatic efforts, aid also included construction of two stadiums in Rwanda and Mozambique as well as parliamentary buildings in Rwanda and Lesotho.

Natural-resource projects made up approximately one-third of pledged and delivered assistance to Africa between 2001 and 2011. In 2004 and 2007, Africa accounted for more than 60 percent of worldwide pledged and delivered FAGIA natural-resource totals, and in 2008 for almost half of China's global annual natural-resource development funding. Given the natural wealth of Africa, Chinese natural-resource development projects there varied significantly by resource type. Oil was the largest resource by program size and frequency. Other resource projects in the region included gold in Eritrea and Zimbabwe, platinum in Zimbabwe and South Africa, diamonds in Zimbabwe, uranium in Niger, and aluminum in Egypt.

"Other" FAGIA, such as debt relief and technical assistance, comprised the smallest share of African-bound aid since 2007. This category of FAGIA also underwent shifts in project types between 2001 and 2011.

Assessment

African-bound assistance has undergone rapid transformations. Prior to 2004, the majority of aid was in the form of debt cancellation. Following 2004, a mix of infrastructure and natural-resource development programs came to dominate FAGIA with Africa. Infrastructure remained the major portion of annual assistance until 2011, and infrastructure and natural-resource programs appear to be complementary. Of the African countries receiving large amounts of funding for natural-resource development, most receive appreciable infrastructure funding as well. Natural-resource programs generally precede infrastructure programs. We conclude that this mix of infrastructure and natural-resource programs appears to follow Chinese needs: Once mineral extraction agreements are in place, China seeks to provide infrastructure funds to meet local development needs to deliver resources.

Middle East

FAGIA in the five Middle East countries—Iran, Iraq, Afghanistan, Jordan, and Turkey—made up 16 percent of the global cumulative pledged assistance and 10 percent of the cumulative delivered assistance. Most aid was directed at developing the energy sector in Iran and Iraq. In Iran, most assistance was used to finance oil and gas projects as well as construction of a railway. Unlike other Middle East countries whose major deals were either in infrastructure building or energy exploration, Iraq received two major debt cancellations by China during the past ten years, totaling $12 billion.

Pledged and Delivered FAGIA: Scale, Trends, and Assessment

Pledged FAGIA

FAGIA pledges to the Middle East increased from $123 million in 2010 to $52 billion in 2011 (the red bars in Figure 5.5). On average, this resulted in an average year-on-year growth of 27 times in the past ten years, albeit with considerable fluctuations. Iran received $88 billion, 83 percent of the total pledged assistance in the region. China signed several major agreements with Iran in 2011, including a $13 billion contract for the construction of eight railway lines to increase the bilateral trade and a $12 billion agreement for oilfield development.[4] The largest deal in the region was a $16 billion investment promised by the CNOOC in 2006 to develop a gas field and a liquefied natural gas plant.

Delivered FAGIA

Annual delivered aid increased from $151 million in 2001 to $6.8 billion in 2010, the last year that our data shows the Middle East receiving delivered assistance. The increase was sporadic and mainly driven by large deals such as Iraq's debt write-offs. As in other regions, the Middle East's share of delivered (rather than pledged) assistance was

---

[4] There was little information about what kind of trade this railroad network was for. But based on the components of China's imports from Iran, we assume this trade-based infrastructure aid merged with other oil and gas development assistance to Iran.

Figure 5.5
Annual and Cumulative Estimates of Pledged and Delivered FAGIA to the Middle East

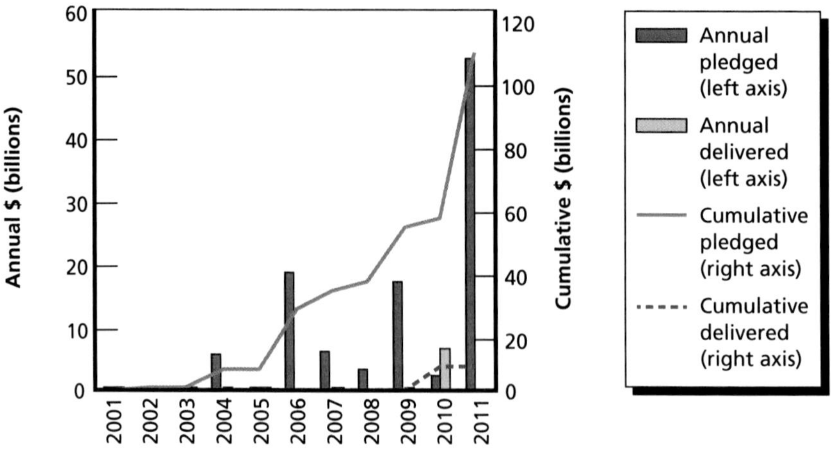

RAND *RR118-5.5*

low; by the end of the decade, only 7 percent of the total pledged aid had been delivered. In most years, the share of delivered assistance was less than 2 percent, which could be attributed to the Middle East's uncertain political and military situations. The only time annual deliveries exceeded annual pledges was in 2010, when a $6.8 billion debt was canceled for Iraq.

Assessment

Most large FAGIA pledges in this region aligned with China's global resource strategy, focused on oil exploration and production in the Middle East. Given that China's demand for oil has increased dramatically in the past ten years, the Middle East became one of China's top choices for energy supply. Since 2006, there have been at least 16 multibillion-dollar pledged assistance projects to the Middle East, nearly all of which were targeted at oil and gas development.

Categories and Purposes of FAGIA Projects: Elaboration and Assessment

Natural-resource development comprises most pledged and delivered aid to the Middle East (Figure 5.6). From 2001 to 2011, the cumulative pledged and delivered resource projects reached $78 billion, which accounted for 25 percent of the total global resource development projects. These programs typically started with assistance unrelated to energy and infrastructure, such as debt relief and financial development, and shifted to the expansion of oil and gas investments starting in 2006. As Figure 5.5 indicates, there were three spikes in pledged assistance—in 2006, 2009, and 2011—that were mainly fueled by the surges for energy development from China's SOEs, e.g. CNPC and CNOOC.

Infrastructure made up a small percentage of the total program in the Middle East until a railroad project was launched in 2011; the share of infrastructure assistance then comprised 40 percent of the pledged and delivered assistance. It is worth noting that in 2002, the Middle East's infrastructure support and "other" forms of assistance each accounted for more than 70 percent of the global share, but that after 2002 there was a sharp decline in the share of infrastructure assistance that the Middle East received, as energy and natural-resource investments became the new focus.

Other FAGIA project categories, including economic development and humanitarian assistance, were usually less than $100 million and were distributed evenly in the region. Large proportions of "other" assistance went to debt cancellation to help rebuild Iraq after the removal of Saddam Hussein. After 2003, China cancelled 80 percent of Iraqi debt. This includes a $6.8 billion debt reduction in 2010 and a $5.8 billion debt write-off in 2004.

Assessment

Natural-resource and energy-oriented assistance for Iran and Iraq dominated aid in the Middle East. These programs continue to grow in accord with China's global energy strategy. For example, China has made several investments on Iran's Azadegan field, after SINOPEC in 2007 developed Yadavaran, an oil field near the border of Iraq.

Figure 5.6
Annual Pledged Plus Delivered FAGIA Estimates to Middle East by Category, 2001–2011

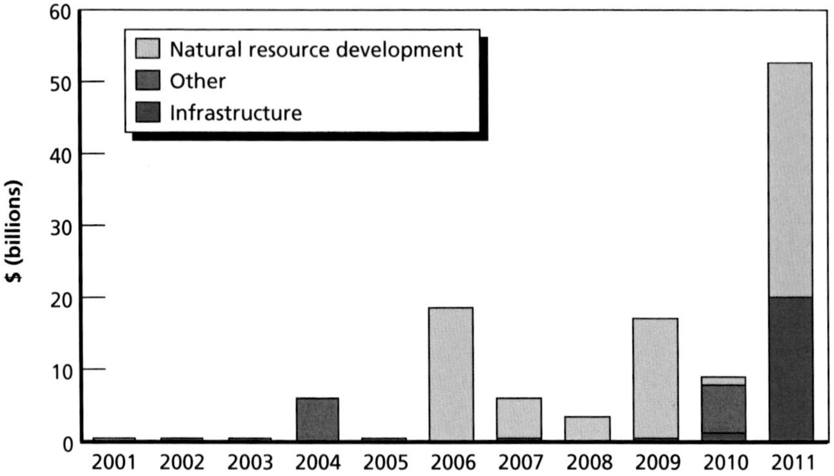

RAND *RR118-5.6*

South Asia

The total FAGIA provided to Pakistan, India, Sri Lanka, Nepal, and Bangladesh in South Asia accounted for 11 percent of the global cumulative pledged assistance and 10 percent of the cumulative delivered assistance between 2001 and 2011. Most aid pledged for South Asia was for infrastructure and financial aid, a striking difference from other regions, where natural-resource development dominated the programs. This anomaly is due to South Asia's limited natural-resource deposits.

Pledged and Delivered FAGIA: Scale, Trends, and Assessment

Pledged FAGIA

From 2003 to 2011, the amount of pledged aid showed significant fluctuation between $0.5 billion and $33 billion, with an average annual increase of five times (the red and purple indicators in Figure 5.7). The sharp increase was led by two major undertakings: 1) an economic development package signed in 2006 that includes building a seaport, oil refineries, and agricultural advancement; and 2) a $15 billion agreement signed in 2010 by China Three Gorges Corporation for the construction of two hydropower projects starting from 2015. Among South Asia countries, Pakistan was the most prominent aid recipient in the past decade, receiving $66 billion, or 87 percent of the regional total aid. Sri Lanka ran a distant second with $5 billion and Nepal rounded out the top three with $2 billion. While Pakistan obtained its largest deals in 2006 and 2010, most other countries secured their largest pledged assistance project in 2011. For example, Nepal obtained a $1.6 billion loan for a hydropower project.

Delivered FAGIA

The delivered assistance has increased significantly, from $70 million in 2001 to $3.6 billion in 2011, with an average year-on-year growth of 30 times. This was entirely driven by the loans for large infrastructure projects in 2011. Given that only 8 percent of the total was actually delivered, this number was one of the lowest in our regional analysis. While some countries in South Asia received proportionally lower shares of delivered aid than others, Sri Lanka, which describes China as

Figure 5.7
Annual and Cumulative Estimates of Pledged and Delivered FAGIA to South Asia

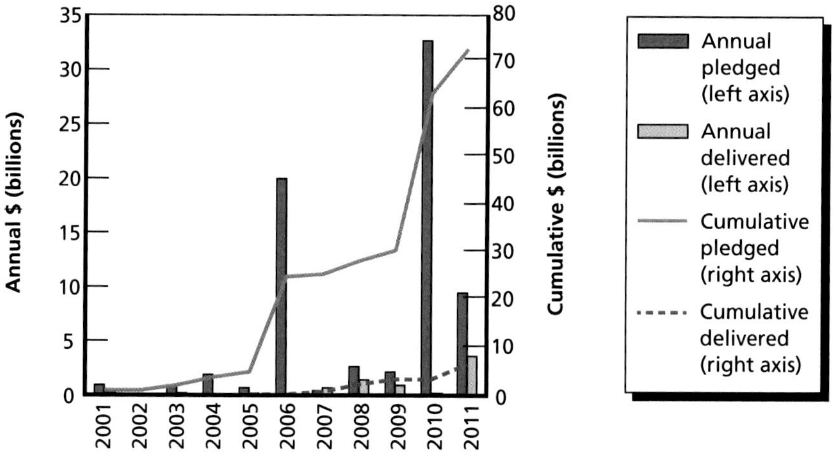

RAND *RR118-5.7*

its largest lender, had 65 percent of its total pledged assistance fulfilled. By contrast, Pakistan only received 6 percent of total aid pledged.

Assessment

China's infrastructure-focused assistance to South Asia was probably driven by the demand side. Unlike Africa and Latin America, South Asia is not a region with rich natural wealth. And China's imports from South Asia mostly comprise agricultural products and raw materials. Therefore, in considering assistance programs to South Asia, China's evident concern may have been related to balancing the power among the South Asian countries, rather than searching for natural resources. The shift of delivered assistance after 2006 could be explained by a combination of economic and political reasons in Pakistan. The Free Trade Agreement between China and Pakistan took effect in July 2007 and the Pakistani election occurred in 2008—and $1 billion in financial assistance was pledged during the new Pakistani president's November 2008 visit to China.

Categories and Purposes of FAGIA Projects: Elaboration and Assessment

Infrastructure-related projects accounted for most FAGIA to South Asia (Figure 5.8). From 2001 to 2011, 17 percent of the China's global infrastructure assistance was allocated to South Asia. Most of the delivered assistance was designated for telecommunication and general economic development projects, which accounted for more than 50 percent of South Asia's total delivered aid from China.

Pledged aid for natural-resource projects was minuscule for the first half of the decade; 2010 marked a shift in focus, with funding pledged for several power plant projects in Pakistan ($14 billion), India ($1 billion) and Sri Lanka ($0.9 billion) from 2010 to 2011. Despite some challenges in the composition of economic development packages, China's assistance mostly followed a four-year cycle and aimed to improve bilateral relationships between the two countries.

Other types of assistance programs include improvement in telecommunication, construction of a fertilizer factory and several multi-billion-dollar projects in housing and general economic development.

Figure 5.8
Annual Pledged Plus Delivered FAGIA Estimates to South Asia by Category, 2001–2011

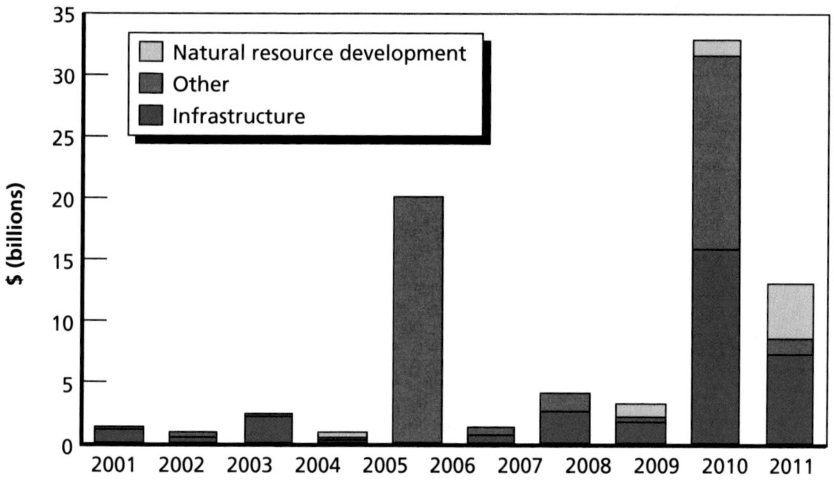

RAND *RR118-5.8*

The largest was a $20 billion trade and economic co-operation agreement signed with Pakistan in 2006, which accounted for 88 percent of the global total FAGIA in that category for that year. Another notable transaction was a $500 million purchase of Pakistani sovereign debt in November 2008.

Assessment

Most programs for South Asia focused on building infrastructure to advance the economic cooperation between China and South Asia. Factoring in the unique political relationship between China and Pakistan, it's not surprising that most aid for the region went to Pakistan exclusively.

Central Asia

Our analysis of Central Asia covers five countries: Kazakhstan, Kyrgyzstan, Uzbekistan, Tajikistan, and Turkmenistan. Central Asia received the least assistance of any region in the past decade, accounting for only 2 to 5 percent of the global energy and infrastructure assistance programs that China distributed in these years. Most of the assistance was offered to fund oil, natural gas, and mining projects. In recent years, regional cooperation organizations such as the Shanghai Cooperation Organisation (SCO) played a major role in increasing China's multilateral trade with the region,[5] which resulted in several major FAGIA agreements for regional infrastructure and natural-resource development.

Pledged and Delivered FAGIA: Scale, Trends, and Assessment

Pledged FAGIA

FAGIA pledges to Central Asia increased from $27 million in 2001 to $7.8 billion in 2011 (Figure 5.9). This was an annual growth of 47 times, led by a sharp increase from $1.4 billion in 2008 to $6.3 billion in 2009. The key drivers for this increase were several large projects for constructing oil and gas pipelines and exploration of copper mines.

Three countries dominated pledges to the region: Kyrgyzstan and Uzbekistan were each offered about $7 billion, and Kazakhstan was offered $5.6 billion.

Delivered FAGIA

FAGIA deliveries increased as FAGIA pledges did. According to the L-N data, annual deliveries increased from $3 million in 2001 to $284 million in 2005 and remained at that level until 2010, when the total amount reached $1 billion. Along with the astonishing growth rate, programs also exhibited an uneven growth distribution among various categories. In particular, energy and resource-related projects had higher delivery rates than any other programs. Some noteworthy deliveries included the two copper-exploration loans provided to Kazakhstan in 2009 and 2011, which gave Kazakhstan the largest delivered share of pledged aid over the past ten years. By the end of the decade, more than 40 percent of its cumulative pledged assistance was fulfilled.

---

[5] The SCO is an intergovernmental international organization founded in June 2001. Its member states include China, Russia, Kazakhstan, Kyrgyzstan, Tajikistan, and Uzbekistan. Its goals are to increase mutual understanding and cooperation in areas such as politics, trade, science and technology, energy, tourism, and environmental protection.

Figure 5.9
Annual and Cumulative Estimates of Pledged and Delivered FAGIA to Central Asia

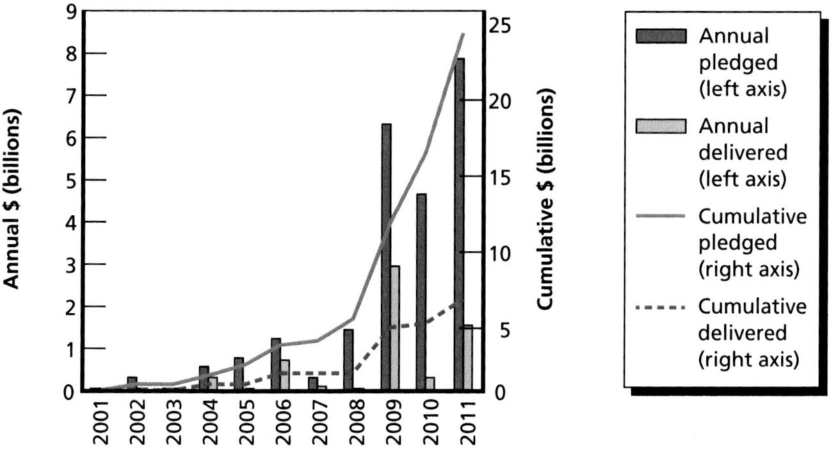

RAND *RR118-5.9*

Assessment

The SCO has played a critical role in China's strategies in Central Asia. Several deals were initiated by SCO agreements in the ten years examined, most of which were small—usually less than $100 million. This trend was drastically altered after a 2010 proposal from the Chinese government for financing $8 billion for the SCO Development Bank to invest in projects related to energy, natural-resource development and basic infrastructure.

Categories and Purposes of FAGIA Projects: Elaboration and Assessment

Natural-resource development in Central Asia showed dramatic increases in 2009, when several significant oil and copper projects were initiated (Figure 5.10). Although the FAGIA share for infrastructure remained low in most years, exceptions appeared in 2006 and 2010, when two multibillion-dollar contracts were signed to finance the development of electricity infrastructure. When comparing resource and infrastructure categories with the "other" project category, the latter not only remained relatively small in the amount of pledged aid, but the share percentage has been steadily decreasing for the past ten years. Such programs include financial support and technical assistance, amounting to less than $500 million each.

Assessment

FAGIA for each country exhibited a unique development focus. For example, most of Kazakhstan's aid was for oil and copper development, while Kyrgyzstan received two large deals for building two hydropower plants. Uzbekistan recently obtained one large natural gas investment, and Tajikistan's relatively small FAGIA was focused on constructing physical infrastructure. In fact, a large proportion of the aid was signed to the entire region as packages, most of which were initiated within the SCO framework. One example is the aforementioned $8 billion fund to the SCO development bank. While the goal of this fund is to promote the multilateral economic cooperation within the SCO member states, it is difficult to tell whether the aid was allocated more to one country or another.

Figure 5.10
Annual Pledged Plus Delivered FAGIA Estimates to Central Asia by Category, 2001–2011

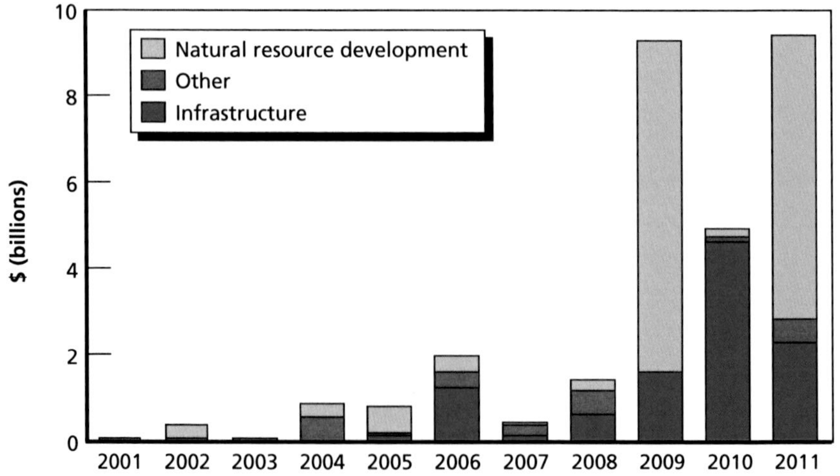

RAND *RR118-5.10*

East Asia

East Asia as we consider it includes 12 nations: Mongolia, North Korea, Cambodia, Philippines, Thailand, Laos, Indonesia, Malaysia, East Timor, Myanmar, Singapore, and Vietnam. This region ranked third among the six regions studied in this report in cumulative pledged assistance. The types of aid deployed to East Asia reflected a more balanced approach than other regions. East Asia was the second-largest destination for infrastructure, the fourth-largest destination for natural-resource funds, and the second largest destination for other forms of assistance. Chinese engagement in East Asia lacked an overarching multilateral structure to coordinate aid, such as the SCO provided in Central Asia, and the China-Africa summits provided in Africa.

Food and fuel transfers from China to North Korea are not included in the aid that is the focus of this study. These in-kind transfers have been part of a longer legacy of China's direct support for North Korea.

Pledged and Delivered FAGIA: Scale, Trends, and Assessment

Pledged FAGIA

As with other regions, cumulative pledged aid increased rapidly, from $16 million in 2001 to $107 billion in 2011 (Figure 5.11). Pledged funds to this region had strong growth, with an annual increase of $10 billion and especially large increases in 2008, 2010, and 2011. Long-term FAGIA-funded infrastructure projects were the primary drivers of this trend.

Delivered FAGIA

Delivered aid comprised only 5 percent of total aid in East Asia between 2001 and 2011. Yearly growth of delivered assistance varied significantly, with four of the ten years posting annual decreases. There were also two significantly different trends in delivered assistance between North Asia (Mongolia and North Korea) and Southeast Asia. North Asian countries had minimal levels of delivered funds, totaling only $9 million between 2001 and 2011. Southeast Asian countries had significantly higher levels of delivered aid, totaling $5.87 billion during this period. Most of these delivered programs focused on infrastruc-

Figure 5.11
Annual and Cumulative Estimates of Pledged and Delivered FAGIA to East Asia

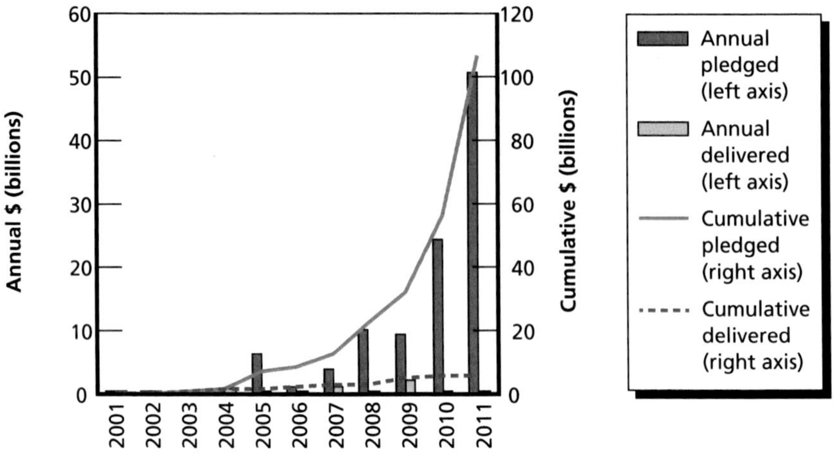

RAND *RR118-5.11*

ture and natural-resource development. The largest of these included \$1 billion for construction of the Hatgyi Dam in Myanmar, and a \$1.9 billion investment by the China Investment Corporation, a Chinese sovereign wealth fund, into an Indonesian coal mining company.

Assessment

Pledged assistance dominated Chinese engagement throughout East Asia. This was due to large amounts of pledged aid for infrastructure projects and other development assistance between 2001 and 2011. Examples include an \$11 billion investment pledged by China's State Grid Corporation to fund the Sarawak Corridor of renewable energy in Malaysia, and \$16.1 billion pledged in 2010 and 2011 as part of the trade and economic agreements between Indonesia and China.

Categories and Purposes of FAGIA Projects: Elaboration and Assessment

The two primary categories of FAGIA to East Asia were infrastructure and "other," with natural resources comprising approximately 15 percent of pledged and delivered aid to the region (Figure 5.12). This contrasts with other regions, which are typically dominated by natural-resource and infrastructure FAGIA. As with the estimates of deliveries, distinct trends were evident among North Asian and South Asian nations. Among North Asian nations, economic development funds dominated pledged and delivered FAGIA prior to 2006. In four of the six following years, infrastructure comprised at least 90 percent of pledged and delivered aid in North Asia. Among Southeast Asian nations, the share of infrastructure aid began at 90 percent of pledged and delivered aid in 2001, dropped to 43 percent of total aid in 2005, and then averaged 54 percent of total aid between 2006 and 2011. The remaining funds focused on a mix of natural-resource and "other" FAGIA.

Infrastructure projects were scattered across several countries and project types. Among North Asian nations, the largest disbursements occurred in 2011 for two infrastructure projects in North Korea, one that developed the Dandong port ($7.1 billion) and another that funded docks, roadways, and power plants in North Korea's Rason SEZ ($2 billion). Projects among Southeast Asian countries included two hydropower plants in Myanmar ($350 million) a hydropower plant in Indonesia ($1 billion), four rail projects spread among Laos, Myanmar, and the Philippines ($8 billion), and construction of a senate building for Cambodia ($2 million).

Other FAGIA was focused on economic- and trade-development projects, a currency swap, and technical assistance. Economic-development projects were split between North Korea and Indonesia, with North Korea receiving pledged funding of approximately $2.1 billion. Indonesia received pledged funding of $16.1 billion for economic- and trade-development projects. A currency swap was executed between China and Thailand in 2011, amounting to $10.8 billion. Most technical assistance was distributed among Indonesia, North Korea, and Laos.

Natural-resource FAGIA to East Asia was for a variety of minerals. Examples of this included a $5 billion investment to support biodiesel in Indonesia in 2008, a $1.9 billion investment in an Indonesian

Figure 5.12
Annual Pledged Plus Delivered FAGIA Estimates to East Asia by Category, 2001–2011

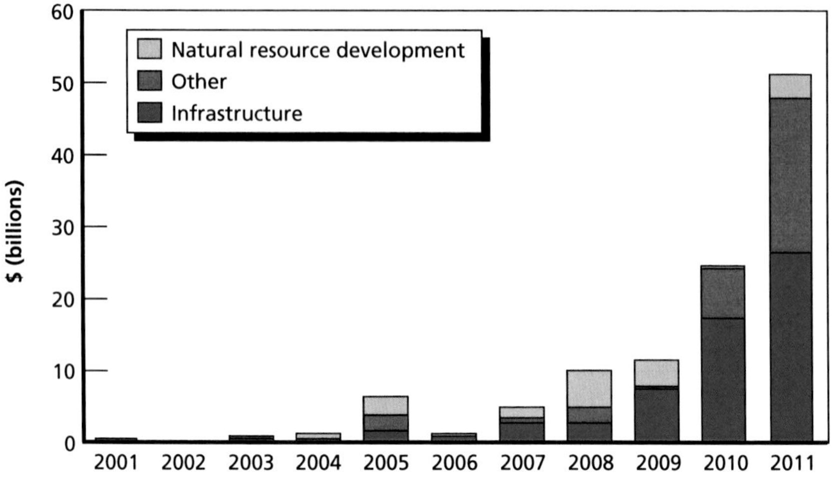

RAND *RR118-5.12*

coal mining company in 2009, and a $1 billion investment for gold and copper exploration in the Philippines in 2009.

Assessment

In both North Asia and Southeast Asia, infrastructure and "other" projects constituted the largest proportion of FAGIA. These programs appear to be largely driven by needs of the recipient country. There were notable exceptions, however, that were complementary with China's wishes. The most prominent of these was a $2.4 billion loan to construct an oil and gas pipeline across Myanmar in 2010, and a $7 billion loan to construct a railway linking the Laotian capital to China in 2011. Chinese medical assistance to Cambodia and Vietnam sought to prevent the spread of SARS in 2003 and avian flu in 2007.

CHAPTER SIX

Inferences, Insights, and Related Issues

China's FAGIA grew rapidly during the first decade of the 21st century, reaching a substantial level by 2011. In 2001, the pledges were slightly below $2 billion, thereafter increasing by an average amount of about $20 billion annually, and reaching a level of $189 billion in 2011. While the scale of aid deliveries also has been rising (albeit not as substantially), financial resources available to and used by China to meet these obligations have been ample. According to IMF data covering China's capital accounts, current official transfers (including credits but excluding "exceptional financing") have remained well above deliveries throughout the period, while displaying a trend that is closely similar to that of deliveries.[1]

Infrastructure projects comprised 40 percent of these pledged amounts, and resource-development projects another 42 percent, with the remaining 18 percent divided among a variety of "other" types of assistance. These "other" types of assistance included debt purchased or forgiven by China, humanitarian and medical aid, technical assistance, and "in-kind" assistance, including food aid. These instances of China's FAGIA consisted largely of "one-off" efforts relating to particular circumstances and particular bilateral relations between China and a recipient country, rather than being regular components of China's regional or global FAGIA programs.

[1] See Appendix B. The IMF data in the appendix charts also show that other foreign assets accumulated by China during this period are ample to provide financing for the pledges as they materialize in deliveries.

As discussed in Chapter Four, cumulative delivered aid was 9.4 percent of cumulative pledged assistance. As previously noted, there are several reasons for the shortfall of deliveries. Both infrastructure and resource projects entail complex details of design, engineering, organization, and management, and hence require long lead times preceding deliveries until completion. Furthermore, since the scale of FAGIA rose sharply after 2008, many deliveries have yet to accrue.

To allow for these considerations, we developed a simple model to express deliveries in 2007–2011 as a six-year lagged function of aid pledged in 2001–2005. The results tend to confirm the expected lag in project deliveries.[2]

China's assistance obligations include provision of funding, technical assistance, equipment, and management. Recipient obligations include providing access to sites for exploration, drilling, and mining, for infrastructure construction, and for exporting resource products to China to service the loans.

While these obligations assure that each side has ample stakes in the endeavor, significant risks remain for both sides. Resource projects may progress more slowly than expected; hence compensatory commodity exports to China may lag. Market prices prevailing at the time of compensatory exports to China may decline below expectations at the time FAGIA agreements were signed.[3] There may be leakages of these exports to importing countries that are unintended—and perhaps undesired—by China. The United States may be among the latter and, in any event, would stand to benefit as a major importer of relatively homogeneous commodities whose supplies are being boosted (and prices lowered) by China's FAGIA programs.

---

[2] $D = \alpha(P) + \beta(T) + \gamma(R)+C$, where D=deliveries in succeeding years, 2007–2011; P= annual pledges in preceding years, 2001–2005; T and R control for fixed effects of years and regions, respectively; and C is the constant. The coefficient, α (0.73, for the lagged pledges) is significant at a 0.05 level, t-value is 2.6,(Prob.F=0.023,R)^2=0.6, adj. R^2=-.4, C=2.2E+09.

[3] This can result in insufficient revenues to service original FAGIA loans, even if resource projects proceed on schedule. Some of the loan agreements are ambiguous as to whether the relevant commodity prices are those prevailing at the time agreements were signed, at the time of commodity loadings, or at the time of delivery. See Downs, 2011.

Recipients of China's aid, as well as the Chinese donor, are exposed to unanticipated risks. For example, imported Chinese equipment may be shoddy, Chinese or indigenous project personnel may be corrupt, or may be corrupted by circumstances and incentives attendant to the programs. Also, project implementation may entail human-rights abuses with adverse repercussions for either or both the recipient and China.[4]

While some of the infrastructure projects are complementary to the resource development projects, more may reflect priority interests of the recipient countries. At the same time, most resource-development projects likely reflect priority interests of China, stemming from its heavy demands for fossil fuels and ferrous and nonferrous metals consequent to its rapid economic growth, perhaps reinforced by a possible diminution of China's domestic supplies and uncertain availabilities from external sources.

It is also likely that some of the infrastructure development may comport with other Chinese national interests. Specifically, improvements and expansion of port facilities in East Africa may enable porting rights and logistic support for elements of the PLA Navy that are currently engaged in patrol missions in the Indian Ocean to counter piracy and to protect sea lanes of communication to and from the Middle East.

Decisions about the project composition of FAGIA are mainly reached through bilateral negotiations between China and each of the 93 recipient countries. In two regions, however, China has immersed its aid programs in a multilateral regional framework. In Africa, the multilateral framework is the triennial China-Africa summit; in Central Asia, it is the SCO.[5] Consequently, the agenda of these meetings generally include discussion of FAGIA. Whether the ensuing discussion in the multilateral meetings affects what is done by China or by FAGIA recipients is not clear.

---

4 See "Deal with Galamsey Operators—Chinese Government," *Ghanaweb,* June 27, 2012. Abuses by Chinese contractors were cited in Ghana and Nigeria, and acknowledged by a member of the CCP Central Committee in a recent Ghanaian conference.

5 See Chapter Five of this report.

The large size of China's programs provides a rough indicator of China's priorities and interests among the recipient regions and countries. By 2011, China's cumulative pledged assistance to 17 countries in Latin America was $186 billion, including as well the largest share of natural-resource development projects among the six regions. Africa received a cumulative total of $175 billion pledged FAGIA distributed among 50 countries.[6] In any event, some recent survey evidence suggests that China may evoke some degree of acknowledgment and perhaps influence in recipient regions as a result of its FAGIA programs.[7] Table 6.1 shows the ten countries receiving the largest amounts of aid from 2001 to 2011.

Table 6.1
Largest Recipients of China's Cumulative Pledged FAGIA, 2001–2011 ($ billions)

Country	$(billions)
Venezuela	106
Iran	89
Nigeria	72
Pakistan	66
Brazil	40
Indonesia	38
Argentina	24
Ghana	22
Malaysia	14
Thailand	13

[6] We have not attempted to normalize the aggregate figures—for example, by population, GDP, per capita GDP, trade, or any other plausible base. In follow-on work, we may pursue this further to see if it suggests anything about China's priorities among countries and regions.

[7] According to a recent BBC global survey, "opinions of China's influence are positive in much of Africa and Latin America, but mostly negative in the United States, everywhere in Europe, as well as in India, Japan, and South Korea." Cited in Joseph S. Nye, Jr., "China's Soft Power Deficit?" *Wall Street Journal*, May 9, 2012. The BBC poll also shows predominantly positive views of China prevailing in Pakistan and Indonesia—large recipients of China's aid.

Future Prospects for China's Foreign FAGIA

Is the scale of China's FAGIA likely to rise, fall, or remain the same in the coming years? In the broad sweep of events and based on the major uncertainties surrounding China's political economy, some factors would tend to sustain or even increase the scale of FAGIA, while others would reduce it.

For example, policymakers confronting a slowing of China's annual GDP growth rate by 3 percent or more might view maintaining or even increasing aid as a valuable stimulus for exports (with the possibly added appeal of being "off-budget" because it is mainly financed by bank lending), and a way of avoiding or reducing unemployment and the possible social unrest that might otherwise ensue. Moreover, if Chinese domestic supplies of fossil fuels and key minerals are further depleted while industrial demands for them continue to grow, incentives may also grow to expand supplies through FAGIA agreements in some of the developing countries and regions.

On the other hand, other factors may tend to diminish pledges of assistance by China. Several competing claimants on domestic, government-financed resources may view reductions of FAGIA as a way of freeing resources to effectuate their claims. The PLA is one major claimant; others include State Council members concerned with the severe income disparities between the rich, dynamic eastern provinces and the poorer and slower-growing central and western ones—the members warn that such disparities might ignite unrest. Yet another factor tending toward diminution may be depletion of the most promising opportunities for finding and developing natural resources in the emerging market countries, absent major new geologic findings or technological advances that enable fuller exploitation of deposits that are already known.[8]

When this cauldron of conflicting ingredients is juxtaposed with our limited understanding of the FAGIA decisionmaking process, no clear answer emerges on the programs' future scale. The emergent

---

[8] These conjectures reflect conversations the authors have had with interlocutors in China, although they are uncorroborated.

bottom line is simply that this matter will command serious attention by China's new leadership and the developing world over the next several years.

While the future of pledged FAGIA is complicated and uncertain, we can use the lagged-function described earlier to estimate deliveries to be expected in the next five years, (2012–2016), based on aid pledges made in the prior 2006–2010 period. We estimate that FAGIA deliveries during the forthcoming five years will be about $338 billion.[9] This is apart from additional assistance programs that China is likely to have pledged since 2011, and may pledge in the future.

Some Related Issues: Confucius Institutes and Arms Transfers

China's Confucius Institutes (CI) and its arms transfer (AT) programs are located at nearly opposite ends of the "soft power/hard power" spectrum that is sometimes used to characterize these instruments.[10] Nonetheless, both have connections with FAGIA, although the connections between them differ and are somewhat tenuous for both. Neither of these programs has been of direct concern in the research described in this report. Consequently, the observations we can make about them are correspondingly limited.

Between 2004 and 2010, China established 322 CIs in 96 countries, including most FAGIA recipients and most countries in the European Union. Additionally, the CIs have active programs under way in the United States at 48 universities, including the University of Chicago, UCLA, Michigan, and Purdue, as well as in the Chicago Public

---

[9] The $338 billion estimate results from multiplying the annual FAGIA pledges in each of the 2006–2010 years by the lagged-variable coefficient (.73), adding the constant, and summing.

[10] For more on soft power and tools of soft power, see Joseph S. Nye, Jr., *Soft Power: The Means to Success in World Politics*, Public Affairs, 2005; Joseph S. Nye, Jr., and Wang Jisi, "Hard Decisions on Soft Power: Opportunities and Difficulties for Chinese Soft Power," *Harvard International Review*, Vol. 31, No. 2, 2009.

School system and the China Institute in New York.[11] The CI programs principally focus on Chinese language instruction in the host countries and provide information about Chinese culture through media materials—literature, films, DVDs, CDs—that impart elements of traditional Chinese culture replete with the attributes mentioned in Chapter Two. The CIs also assist China's domestic efforts to finance and expand education of undergraduate students and graduate students from foreign countries. Although CI funding levels are not publicized, they are negligible compared to the scale of FAGIA. Nevertheless, they share with FAGIA the aim of enhancing China's appeal, attractiveness, and influence in the global arena—hence, its "soft power."

The possibly tenuous connection between economic assistance and China's arms transfers can be formulated as a question: Is there any link between aid recipients and China's arms sales or transfers to selected countries? China is a rising global supplier of arms to developing countries, although it is still far below the two largest suppliers. Between 2002 and 2009, the U.S. share of global arms deliveries to all developing countries was 35 percent ($64 billion); that for Russia was 22 percent ($40 billion), while China's share was 6 percent ($11.5 billion). China was the fifth-largest supplier (also trailing the United Kingdom [UK] and France) from 2002 to 2009, becoming the third-largest supplier in 2009, when its arms deliveries to all developing nations exceeded the totals of the UK and France combined.[12]

Perhaps reflecting a loose connection to the priority accorded Africa in the FAGIA data, China was, with Germany, one of the two principal suppliers of arms to that region in the 2006–2009 period, although arms deliveries to Africa by both of these suppliers were quite small ($900 million). On the other hand, China's arms deliveries in this period to Latin America—the other high priority region for China's economic aid—were small relative to China's arms deliveries to East

---

[11] For the U.S. data, see George Mason University, *Confucius Institute at Mason,* web page, undated. For the worldwide data, see Confucius Institutes, *Confucius Institutes in the World,* web page, undated.

[12] Richard Grimmett, *Conventional Arms Transfers to Developing Nations, 2002–2009,* Congressional Research Service, 2010.

Asia and the Middle East (about $3 billion in each of these regions). This would suggest that, if there is any connection between the priorities reflected in China's FAGIA and in its arms transfers, it is tenuous.

APPENDIX A

Data and Methodology

FAGIA data used in this study were developed primarily from the dataset used by CRS for their report.[1] This dataset was originally assembled with assistance from New York University's Robert F. Wagner Graduate School of Public Service in 2007–2008. After expanding both the number of countries and the time frame, our data covered 93 countries in six major regions including Africa, Latin America, East Asia (including Southeast Asia), the Middle East, South Asia, and Central Asia from 2001 to 2011.[2]

A trade-based method was also used to estimate deliveries. This method assumes FAGIA deliveries can be approximated from differences in imports from China to a recipient country over time.

Data were drawn from the IMF's Direction of Trade Statistics, consisting of each country's imports from the world, and each country's imports from China. We estimated yearly FAGIA deliveries by calculating the recipient's imports from China above the recipient's normal China share of its global imports.[3]

---

1 Lum, 2009.

2 Readers who wish to receive the full data set we used may request it by email to wolf@rand.org, xiaowang@rand.org, or ewarner@rand.org.

3 The equation used in this calculation was $CFAP_{delivered,t} = M_{c,t} - Q_{normal,t} * M_{g,t}$ where

$$Q_{normal,t} = \frac{Q_{t-3} + Q_{t-2} + Q_{t-1} + Q_t}{4}$$

$M_{c,t}$ is the annual value of imports from China in year t and $M_{g,t}$ the annual value of total imports from the world for a recipient country in year t.

Unfortunately this method yielded results that were uncorrelated and inconsistent with the L-N estimates. Because of this, we have omitted them from this report.

Search Methods

The primary source of information was from media reports retrieved from the LexisNexis Academic online search tool.[4] First, depending on existing data in the CRS data for a specific country, we define the time frame for collection either from 2001 to 2011 or from 2008 to 2011. Second, we identified 93 countries representative of their respective regions. Next, we tested four different search methods and selected one method for each country based on the number of articles in the search results. To gain a representative sample of the FAGIA for these countries, we limited the number of results to no more than 100 articles per country. Repeat articles were eliminated in search results but were used as cross-references to our data. In the end, we obtained 1,055 news articles for the 93 countries in our study.

When conducting the L-N search, we used different combinations of keywords in the headline, leading paragraph, and the main body. The search strategies used are listed below in descending order of search results. For example, as of February 20, 2012, the number of results for Egypt using methods 1 to 4 was 1,142, 567, 58, and 52, respectively. In most cases Method 3 and Method 4 are our preferred search methods. We use the other two methods where the number of results are too small, e.g. less than 10.

L-N Search Terms:
!=truncation (e.g., lend! retrieves lend and lending)
headline = headline of article
hlead = headline or first paragraph of article
country = the specific recipient country

[4] "LexisNexis® is a leading global provider of content-enabled workflow solutions designed specifically for professionals in the legal, risk management, corporate, government, law enforcement, accounting, and academic markets. LexisNexis originally pioneered online information with its Lexis® and Nexis® services." LexisNexis database homepage, undated. LexisNexis® Academic includes more than 600 major world publications.

(If no command was put before the parenthesis, we search the full text.)

Method 1
hlead((loan! or lend! or grant! or debt or aid or invest! or develop! or infrastructure or assist! or support! or financ! or invest! or agree!) and (china or chinese or PRC) and **country**)
and
($ or millions or trillions or dollars or yuan or billions)

Method 2
hlead((loan! or lend! or grant! or debt or aid or invest! or develop! or infrastructure or assist! or support! or financ! or invest! or agree!) and (china or chinese or PRC) and **country**)
and
hlead($ or millions or trillions or dollars or yuan or billions)

Method 3
headline((loan! or lend! or grant! or debt or aid or invest! or develop! or infrastructure or assist! or support! or financ! or invest! or agree!) and (china or chinese or PRC))
and
hlead(($ or millions or trillions or dollars or yuan or billions) and **country**)

Method 4
headline((loan! or lend! or grant! or debt or aid or invest! or develop! or infrastructure or assist! or support! or financ! or invest! or agree!) and (china or chinese or PRC) and **country**)
and
($ or millions or trillions or dollars or yuan or billions)

Countries

Data was collected on 93 countries in the six regions in our analysis, which include 49 countries in Africa, 17 countries in Latin America, 12 countries in East Asia (including Southeast Asia), five countries in the Middle East, five countries in South Asia, and five countries in

Central Asia. Tables A.1 shows a list of countries we included in this report.

Dimensions

After collecting all data, FAGIA was divided by region, purpose of support (infrastructure, natural-resource development, or "other"), and whether the assistance was delivered or pledged. Table A.2 shows an example of one data entry.

Table A.1
List of Recipient Countries in the FAGIA Database

Africa			Latin America	Middle East	East Asia	South Asia	Central Asia
Algeria	Ethiopia	Niger	Argentina	Afghanistan	Cambodia	Bangladesh	Kazakhstan
Angola	Gabon	Nigeria	Bolivia	Iran	East Timor	India	Kyrgyzstan
Benin	Ghana	Rwanda	Brazil	Iraq	Indonesia	Nepal	Tajikistan
Botswana	Guinea	Senegal	Chile	Jordan	Laos	Pakistan	Turkmenistan
Burundi	Guinea-Bissau	Seychelles	Colombia	Turkey	Malaysia	Sri Lanka	Uzbekistan
Cameroon	Kenya	Sierra Leone	Costa Rica		Mongolia		
Cape Verde	Lesotho	Somalia	Cuba		Myanmar		
Central African Republic	Liberia	South Africa	Dominica		North Korea		
Chad	Libya	Sudan	Ecuador		Philippines		
Comoros	Madagascar	Tanzania	El Salvador		Singapore		
Cong (DRC)	Malawi	Togo	Grenada		Thailand		
Congo (Brazilleville)	Mali	Tunisia	Haiti		Vietnam		
Cote d'Ivoire	Mauritanian	Uganda	Honduras				
Djibouti	Mauritius	Zambia	Mexico				
Egypt	Morocco	Zimbabwe	Peru				
Equatorial Guinea	Mozambique		Uruguay				
Eritrea	Namibia		Venezuela				

Table A.2
Example of Data Entry of China's FAGIA in One Country

Region	Country	Year	Aid in US$	Purpose of Support	Pledged	Description	Source
Africa	Egypt	2010	250 million	Natural-resource development	Yes	A total of 22 agreements were signed between companies from Egypt and Guangdong, China, with total investments of more than $250 million, during a business forum held during one week in 2010.	"Egyptian, Chinese Companies Sign 22 Agreements Worth $250 Million," *Tendersinfo News*, October 24, 2010.

APPENDIX B

International Monetary Fund's International Financial Statistics Data

We compared our L-N delivery data with China's current account balance data drawn from IMF's International Financial Statistics (IFS) database and World Bank data. Three components of the balance of payment are compared here: 1) transfers, 2) loans, and 3) foreign direct investment. The following charts show that between 2004 and 2010, China's transfers and other foreign assets were ample to provide financing for the pledges as they materialized in deliveries. And both the current account data and the L-N deliveries data show similar increases after 2007.

While the IMF/World Bank data only cover loans and transfers that have already been made, our FAGIA estimates also cover pledged financing. Furthermore, the IMF/World Bank data explicitly omit from loans and transfers (as well as from FDI) funding that is provided by what the IMF calls "exceptional financing," whereas our estimates for both deliveries and pledges explicitly include such funding. Specifically, all of the FAGIA financing provided by China's Development Bank and most of that provided by China's Export-Import Bank consist of "exceptional financing" and thus are omitted from the IMF/World Bank data.

In the charts and tables, we have included data showing China's annual current account surpluses for the 2001–2010 decade to show how large these surpluses have been compared to both aid deliveries and pledges.

Table B.1
Comparison Between RAND FAGIA Estimates and IMF/World Bank Balance of Payments Data, 2001–2010

Source	Indicator Name	Currency	Scale	2001	2002	2003	2004	2005	2006	2007	2008	2009	2010
World Bank	Current Account Balance	US Dollars	Billions	17.40	35.42	43.05	68.94	132.38	231.84	353.18	420.57	243.26	237.81
IMF	IIP Assets, Direct Investment Abroad	US Dollars	Billions				52.70	64.49	90.63	115.96	185.69	245.75	310.84
IMF	IIP Assets, Other Investment (loans)	US Dollars	Billions				165.76	216.38	253.85	468.31	552.29	515.36	643.91
IMF	Current Transfers, Credit (Excludes Exceptional Financing)	US Dollars	Billions	99.13	13.80	18.48	24.33	27.73	31.58	42.65	52.57	42.65	49.52
RAND	Deliveries	US Dollars	Billions	00.47	00.04	11.21	1.07	2.66	12.97	2.12	4.64	6.47	17.98
RAND	Deliveries+ Pledges	US Dollars	Billions	22.19	00.75	22.87	19.51	14.24	59.52	29.79	84.76	131.31	186.55

Table B.1—Continued

Source	Indicator Name	Currency	Scale	2001	2002	2003	2004	2005	2006	2007	2008	2009	2010
	Share of current account surplus in the sum of FDI, loans and transfers	US Dollars	Billions				28%	43%	62%	56%	53%	30%	24%

NOTE: IIP = International Investment Position.

Figure B.1
Comparison Between RAND's FAGIA Estimates and IMF/World Bank Balance of Payments Data, 2001–2010

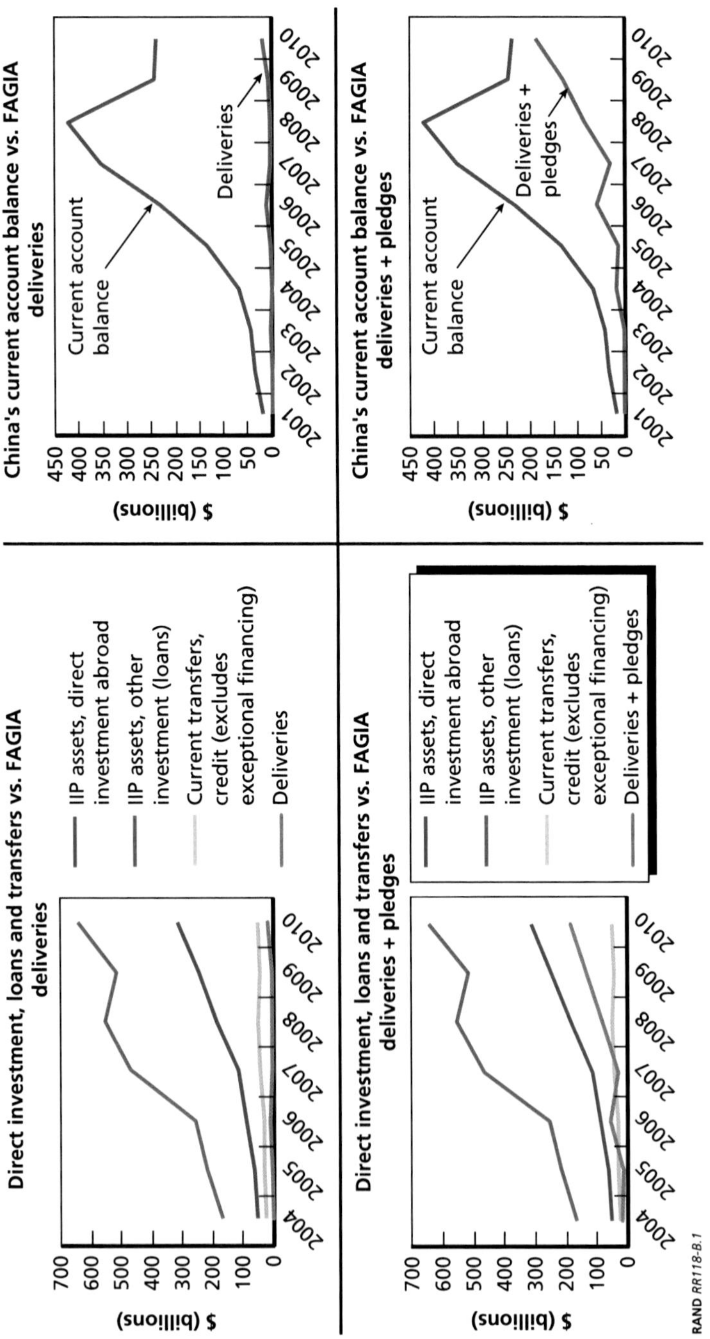

RAND *RR118-B.1*

Figure B.2
Comparison of the Values of China's Current Account Data and L-N-Delivered Assistance Estimates, 2004–2010

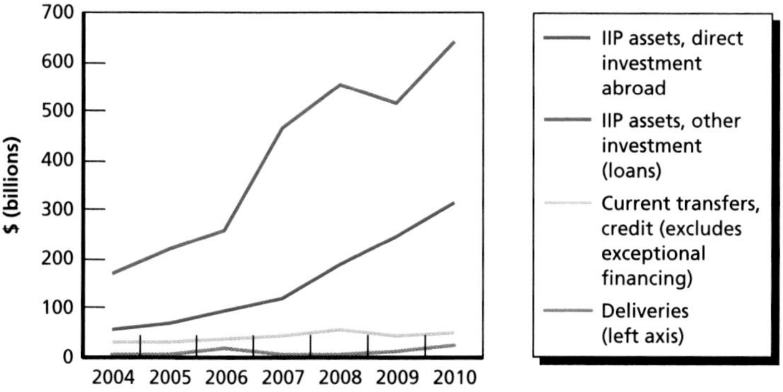

RAND *RR118-B.2*

Finally, it's worth noting that stocks of loans and other assets do not enter into balance of payments data: The latter represent flows; the former are stocks, consisting of accumulations of prior flows. The two relate to one another in the same way that budget deficits (i.e., "flows") relate to debt (i.e., "stocks").

Figure B.3
Comparison of the Trend of China's Current Account Data and L-N-Delivered Assistance Estimates, 2004–2010

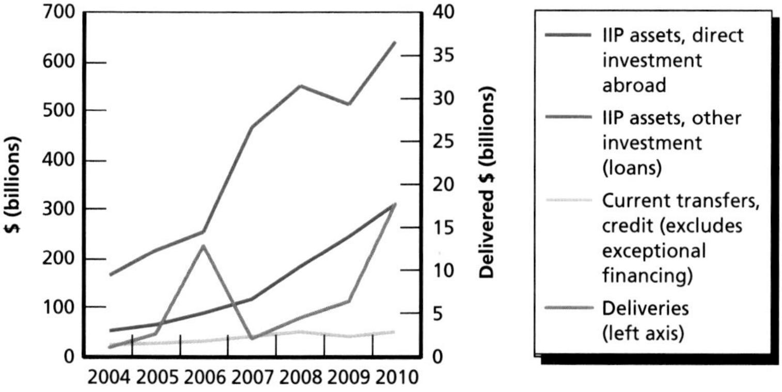

RAND *RR118-B.3*

References

Akramov, Kamiljon T., *Foreign Aid Allocation, Governance, and Economic Growth*, International Food Policy Research Institute, 2012.

Boone, Peter, "Politics and the Effectiveness of Foreign FAGIA," *European Economic Review*, Vol. 40, No. 2, 1996.

Brautigam, Deborah, *The Dragon's Gift: The Real Story of China in Africa*, Oxford, UK: Oxford University Press, 2011.

Burnside, Craig, and David Dollar. "Aid, Policies, and Growth." *American Economic Review*, Vol. 90, No. 4, 2000.

"CDB, SINOPEC and Petrobras Sign $10 Billion Loan-for-Oil Contract," *Global Times*, May 26, 2010.

"China Establishes Diplomatic Relations with the Commonwealth of Dominica," Ministry of Foreign Affairs of the People's Republic of China, March 30, 2004.

"China, Costa Rica Set Up Diplomatic Ties," *China Daily*, June 26, 2007.

Confucius Institutes, *Confucius Institutes in the World,* web page, undated. As of March 10 2012:
http://college.chinese.cn/en/node_1979.htm

Davies, Martyn, Hannah Edinger, Nastasya Tay, and Sanusha Naidu, "How China Delivers Development Assistance to Africa," Centre for Chinese Studies, University of Stellenbosch, 2008.

"Deal with Galamsey Operators—Chinese Government," *Ghanaweb*, June 27, 2012.

Downs, Erica, "Inside China, Inc: China Development Bank's Cross-Border Energy Deals," Brookings Institute, 2011.

Easterly, William, Ross Levine, and David Roodman, *New Data, New Doubts: A Comment on Burnside and Dollar's "Aid, Policies, and Growth" (2000)*, National Bureau of Economic Research, 2003.

"Egyptian, Chinese Companies Sign 22 Agreements Worth $250 Million," *Tendersinfo News*, October 24, 2010.

George Mason University, *Confucius Institute at Mason*, web page, undated. As of March 10, 2012:
http://confucius.gmu.edu

Grimmett, Richard, *Conventional Arms Transfers to Developing Nations, 2002–2009*, Congressional Research Service, 2010.

Hall, Simon, and Xu Wan, "CNPC, SINOPEC, CNOOC Sign Venezuela O&G Deals," *Dow Jones Newswires*, December 3, 2010.

Hubbard, Paul, *Aiding Transparency: What We Can Learn About China Exim Bank's Concessional Loans*, Center for Global Development, 2007.

International Institute for Strategic Studies, *The Military Balance*, 2012.

International Monetary Fund, *SDR Interest Rate Calculation* web page, undated. As of September 2012:
http://www.imf.org/external/np/fin/data/sdr_ir.aspx

Information Office of the State Council, "China's Foreign Aid" white paper, Beijing, April 2011.

LexisNexis database home page, undated. As of January 7, 2012
http://www.lexisnexis.com/

Lloyd, Tim, Mark McGillivray, Oliver Morrissey, and Robert Osei, "Does Aid Create Trade? An Investigation for European Donors and African Recipients," *The European Journal of Development Research*, Vol. 12, No. 1, 2000.

Lum, Thomas, *China's Assistance and Government-Sponsored Investment Activities in Africa, Latin America, and Southeast Asia*, Congressional Research Service, 2009.

Lum, Thomas, Hannah Fischer, Julissa Gomez-Granger, and Anne Leland, *China's Foreign Aid Activities in Africa, Latin America, and Southeast Asia*, Congressional Research Service, 2009.

Mankiw, Gregory, *Macroeconomics*, Worth Publishers, 2012.

Morrisey, Oliver, and Howard White, "Evaluating the Concessionality of Tied Aid," The Manchester School, 1996.

Nye, Joseph S. Jr., and Wang Jisi, "Hard Decisions on Soft Power: Opportunities and Difficulties for Chinese Soft Power," *Harvard International Review*, Vol. 31, No. 2, 2009.

Nye, Joseph S. Jr., *Soft Power: The Means to Success in World Politics*, Public Affairs, 2005.

———, "China's Soft Power Deficit?" *Wall Street Journal*, May 9, 2012.

OECD—*See* Organization for Economic Co-operation and Development.

Organization for Economic Co-operation and Development, *Development Assistance Committee Glossary of Key Terms and Concepts* web page, undated. As of 2012:
http://www.oecd.org/dac/dacglossaryofkeytermsandconcepts.htm

Rajan, G. Raghuram, and Arvind Subramanian, "Aid and Growth: What Does the Cross-Country Evidence Really Show?" NBER Working Paper, No. 11513, Cambridge, Mass.: National Bureau of Economic Research, 2005.

"Timeline: Libor-Fixing Scandal," *BBC*, February 6, 2013.

U.S. Export-Import Bank, *Annual Report*, 2012.

Wagner, Don, "Aid and Trade—An Empirical Study," *Journal of the Japanese and International Economies*, Vol. 17, No. 2, 2003.

Wolf, Charles Jr., *Markets or Governments: Choosing Between Imperfect Alternatives*, MIT Press, 1993.

Wolf, Charles Jr., Brian G. Chow, Gregory S. Jones, and Scott Harold, *China's Expanding Role in Global Merger and Acquisitions Markets*, Santa Monica, Calif.: RAND Corporation, MG-1162-CAPP, 2011. As of June 17, 2013:
http://www.rand.org/pubs/monographs/MG1162.html